MBA IN A DAY 2.0

MBA IN A DAY 2.0

What you would learn at top-tier business schools (if you only had the time!)

STEVEN STRALSER PH.D.

ISBN-13: 9780997532401
ISBN-10: 0997532408
Library of Congress Control Number: 2016943945
Center for Professional Development, Incorporated, The, Phoenix, AZ

A NOTE ABOUT MBA IN A DAY 2.0

The world has changed greatly since *MBA in a DAY* was first published the same year that Google raised $1.67 billion in their initial public offering and Facebook had just launched at Harvard for students only. Ever since, we have collectively recognized, and most of us have been affected by, the codependency of living in an increasingly global economic system. This more recent world has become more digital, more mobile, and more wired, where time is measured not in days, weeks, or months but in milliseconds. This digital economy has changed the way we shop, the way we work, and the way we socialize, and it has touched almost every daily activity.

This updated version of *MBA in a DAY* brings a more digital, more global, more connected world in focus and, with the same easy-to-understand manner, presents critical concepts found in today's top-tier MBA programs and keeps a promise to its readers to be "leading edge."

PREFACE

Of course you can't get an MBA degree in a day—ask anyone who has put in the months and years needed to accomplish this challenging and rewarding achievement. However, this book is where you will find, in basic, easy-to-understand language, MBA concepts and principles that are presented in the gold standard of business education throughout the world—the master of business administration.

The story behind this book comes from my years teaching in a full-time MBA program, where I began to notice something I found very interesting. Every semester, in addition to the "traditional" MBA students who had taken time off from their corporate life to enroll in the MBA program, I would find one or two students who were clearly "outliers" to these mainstream corporate-types—for example, a physician, an attorney, an executive director from a nonprofit organization, or a small-business owner or entrepreneur.

It did not take long to realize this trend was an indicator of an underlying interest and need for these well-educated professionals—well trained in the education of their profession—to learn about the "business side" of their professional lives.

These non–business trained professionals wanted to fill a gap and learn business principles and concepts needed in their professional practices but not taught in medical schools or other professional schools, such as law, engineering, architecture, veterinary, or other highly specialized training programs.

I also realized that for every physician, attorney, architect, or entrepreneur who can take the time to enroll in an MBA program, there are many more who are time-pressed and focused on the day-to-day challenges of running a successful practice, operating a small business, or launching a new venture. These successful professionals would certainly benefit from learning the essential principles and concepts found in the coursework of an MBA program, and it is for them that this book is written.

In this book, you will learn the fundamental concepts and principles that full-time MBA students learn and that also have applicability to professional service providers, small-business owners, and entrepreneurs as well as corporations and industry. These principles and concepts are not industry- or profession-specific—they are classic, strategic, and essential in performing in today's complex economic environment.

This book is organized into four main sections, with relevant chapters in each section.

SECTION I: PEOPLE—MANAGEMENT AND POLICY

CHAPTER 1. HUMAN RESOURCES

Points out that all businesses start with and revolve around people, or "human capital." Discusses how human assets can best be utilized, including personnel selection, training, and development. Covers the regulatory aspects of areas such as discrimination, harassment, and disabilities. Explores hiring and firing practices as well as promotional policies.

CHAPTER 2. ORGANIZATIONAL BEHAVIOR

Describes alternative organizational structures and designs and the advantages and disadvantages of each. Explains how to build and maintain appropriate organizational cultures, including learning organizations that can successfully evolve in response to changing environments. Also discusses building a culture of innovation—what leaders need to know to turn new ideas, products, processes, or services into drivers of profitability and financial sustainability.

CHAPTER 3. LEADERSHIP AND TEAM BUILDING

Catalogs various leadership styles and the advantages and disadvantages of each. Explores the use of teams to maximize efficiency as organizations become increasingly complex and specialized. Sets forth situations in which teams are most successful and unsuccessful, how team members should be selected, how to manage and coordinate teams and develop effective team leaders.

CHAPTER 4. ETHICS

Focuses on decisions that managers are required to make in the context of ever-evolving business mores. Relies upon case studies involving companies such as

Enron to provide graphic guidelines on how to exercise appropriate judgments in decision-making, information disclosures, and financial representations. Additionally, there's an exploration of the company as citizen: corporate social responsibility is more than "being green"…it's a key factor in shaping strategy and long-term profitability.

CHAPTER 5. NEGOTIATION

Examines conflict resolution—understanding processes for reaching agreement on issues facing the organization and its stakeholders. Readers will be instructed on how to prepare for negotiations, set objectives and priorities, and select tactics and fallback positions. Scripts will be presented for various roles and approaches utilized in negotiating and a list of negotiation dos and don'ts will be provided.

SECTION II: MONEY—ECONOMICS, FINANCE, AND ACCOUNTING

CHAPTER 6. ACCOUNTING BASICS

Explains the meaning of the language and importance of consistency in accounting. Discusses the basic principles of tracking revenues, expenses, and results from an organization's activities. Examines accounting alternatives such as cash versus accrual methods, matching revenues with expenses, and the philosophy behind depreciating assets.

CHAPTER 7. FINANCIAL MANAGEMENT

Builds upon the preceding chapter to discuss the importance of financial statements in fiscal management. Presents technical information in clear, understandable language. Teaches readers how to interpret and understand the basic tools of financial management and apply basic accounting principles to determine the financial health of the organization.

CHAPTER 8. ECONOMICS: LOCAL, NATIONAL, AND GLOBAL

Discusses the vocabulary of economics to measure supply and demand. Details how nations, corporations, and individuals efficiently apply scarce resources (macro- and microeconomics). Developing a "global mind-set" and its value in fostering an organization's long-term financial sustainability.

SECTION III: MARKETS AND STRATEGY

CHAPTER 9. MARKETING, STRATEGY, AND COMPETITIVE ANALYSIS

Provides readers with information about how to examine trends and the strengths and weaknesses of their competitors, industries, and the markets where they exist. Explores the forces that shape an organization's competitive environment.

CHAPTER 10. COMMUNICATIONS AND PRESENTATIONS

Provides an overview of how organizations can increase their profits by informing and persuading customers, clients, and stakeholders about the benefits of their products and services. Addresses how and when to use alternatives such as advertising, public relations, direct marketing, and relationship-based promotions. Gives an overview of social media, web-based marketing, and promotion in an increasingly digital world and the ingredients for creating a successful marketing website.

Teaches readers the basics on how to "tell a story" or transmit information to an audience or market. Examines the factors influencing persuasion, the content of presentations and provides a listing of dos and don'ts.

SECTION IV: SYSTEMS AND PROCESSES—MANAGEMENT INFORMATION SYSTEMS

CHAPTER 11. PROJECT MANAGEMENT

Explains how readers can tackle specific projects from start to finish and efficiently manage them. Describes the importance of flexibility and points out companies generally do not operate in a continual process but tend to do things in spurts. Shows readers how to recognize those spurts and manage them efficiently. Discusses how technology is bringing increasing efficiency to project management.

CHAPTER 12. MANAGEMENT INFORMATION SYSTEMS

Explores Management Information Systems and how they help managers organize and make decisions from their data. More simply, effective MIS aids communication and draws on the principle—still true—that people generally accomplish more together than they do apart. The well-accepted concept of collaboration and communication is still at the core of business. Management information systems strive to efficiently collect, format, and communicate information to a wide variety of people.

CHAPTER 13. THE WEB AND THE "INTERNET OF THINGS"

Discusses the essentials for today's cyber environment and technology-driven organization. Explores "Software as a Service" and mobile platform models to harnessing technology for organizational efficiency and effectiveness as well as the use of the Web as a vehicle to improve internal organizational efficiency.

CHAPTER 14. QUALITY MANAGEMENT SYSTEMS

Discusses the most highly regarded measuring devices and the importance of the philosophies behind them in revealing key organizational values. Systems covered include the Six Sigma approach to measure and improve quality within an organization, TQM (Total Quality Management), and CQI (Continuous Quality Improvement), which are used to evaluate performance and organizational competitiveness.

ACKNOWLEDGMENTS

This book would not have been possible without the collaboration and participation by a great team of researchers, writers, and contributors, composed of MBA graduates from Thunderbird School of Global Management, many of whom I had the privilege of teaching and mentoring at this exceptional school that produces well-trained and well-educated managers and leaders of global business and enterprise.

Lenora E. Peppers, MBA-IM, the team leader, is managing director of Kick-Start Marketing and newly appointed executive director of the Thunderbird Independent Alumni Association. Arthur Holcombe, MBA, is managing director of Snupps Ltd. in London. Ronald J. Greene, MBA, is founder and managing partner at Blackrock Consulting Group in Austin Texas. Jaxon Ravens, MBA, is chair of the executive board for the Washington State Democratics. Suchi Patel, MBA, is customer insights manager at Vistaprint in Boston, Massachusetts. Allison Kaiser, MBA, is senior vice president of innovation at CDC Small Business Finance in Oakland, California, and Rachel Neft, MBA-IM, is a marketing manager in the Chicago corporate office of True Value Hardware Company.

Finally, I wish to express my thanks and appreciation to some important women in my life: to my bride, Rosemary, with love and appreciation for signing up for an adventure and for being a great partner as that adventure in life together has been unfolding...to my daughters, Amy and Marcy, you have made me so proud of your own achievements both as moms and wives, and as successful professional women! And, to my awesome grandkids Harrison Neiss, Holly Neiss, Justin Lewis and Noah Lewis, you are all achieving success in your own individual way; I thought about you a lot while writing this book.

DEDICATION

This book is dedicated to my father, Harold, a hero in many ways.

ABOUT THE AUTHOR

Steven Stralser is Professor Emeritus at Thunderbird School of Global Management and received his PhD from the University of Michigan, where he taught Marketing and Marketing Strategy. He holds a BS in Marketing from the University of Arizona and an MBA from Arizona State University.

During fall 1999, he was a Fulbright Senior Scholar, teaching marketing management in the MBA program at the Budapest University of Economic Sciences and Entrepreneurship at the University of Miskolc.

His interests outside academe and the professional world include playing left defenseman for his men's adult ice-hockey team, restoring (and hopefully driving) his 1951 Riley 2.5L RMB Saloon, and sharing adventures with his bride, Rosemary, and their growing-up-fast clan of grandchildren.

TABLE OF CONTENTS

Section I

PEOPLE, MANAGEMENT, AND POLICY

Chapter 1

HUMAN RESOURCES

R ecruiting, hiring, and retaining competent employees has always been an important part of any business. In the business world today, this function has become ever more complex and important. The business environment is forever changing, and managers and human resources departments must be flexible enough to adapt to these changes, including the changing laws, demographics, and business strategies. The typical human resources department usually has two functions:

1. Providing the organization with qualified and well-trained employees for every position
2. Keeping all hiring and employment activities and practices in accordance with all laws and regulations

This chapter will cover the first function; it's well beyond the scope of this book to cover the nuance and complexity of legal issues associated with human resources.

HUMAN RESOURCES PLANNING AND STRATEGY

Just like any other aspect of business management, planning and strategy development are the first items on the agenda when tackling a project. Managers, professionals, and entrepreneurs are often faced with the task of developing a plan for how human resources will be needed to meet short- and long-term goals and objectives. For example, a company is interested in expanding its production capacity with a new plant to serve its western US markets. As part of the strategic planning for this new facility, a human resources component of this expansion will be essential.

In its simplest form, human resource planning starts by conducting an analysis of staffing needs throughout the organization. This could mean either assessing the current staffing requirements or future requirements if changes are expected. In either situation, there are several questions that need to be answered and fully understood prior to the analysis:

1. What is the organization's strategic vision?
2. What are the short-term and long-term goals?
3. Are there any major changes in the market that will impact the organization's future?
4. What changes in staffing requirements, if any, are needed to support the strategic vision of the organization?
5. If changes are needed within the organization, what type of resistance can be expected to the change?

Once these questions are answered, assessing the staffing requirements can be completed.

Assessing the staffing plans involves evaluating the human capacity needed to meet the goals and objectives of the organization, estimating the number of people needed for each department or role, and making adjustments as needed. This process does take a lot of experience and understanding of the specific business, but experienced managers should be able to make good assessments. If the managers are new to the industry, a good benchmark would be comparing the number of employees needed in similar organizations.

Here are some signs that the current staffing needs are not in line with the condition of the organization:

- There are regular breakdowns in the process flows, jeopardizing relationships with clients and customers. These include missed deadlines, increased returns, decreased customer loyalty, and regular administration mistakes.
- There is frequent employee absenteeism and turnover—caused by employees being over-stressed, having poor morale, or looking for other employment.
- Overtime occurs regularly, caused by employees being overworked or given too much responsibility. Overworking employees can lead to burnouts and increased costs in the long run.

Once the staffing plan that meets the current and future plans for the organization is developed, job descriptions can be developed. This process involves analyzing each job in the organization in order to generate a job description and job specifications, and then these are aggregated at a company-wide level. Job descriptions can be a very important management tool in some organizations. Some thought should be put into them due to the nature of employees using job descriptions to define and defend their actions or inactions. Job descriptions can be either a restraint or an open door for employees or teams.

The job analysis involves collecting sufficient information to form a complete understanding of what is entailed to perform the job. A job description lists the activities that the employee performs, as well as the skills and qualities that are needed to successfully meet the job objectives. Think of this stage of human resource planning as if you were a newly appointed coach of an expansion football franchise. You would identify first the positions you would need to complete the roster, then the qualities you would like for each player, specific to each position.

Once the job analysis and job descriptions are determined, this information can then be aggregated to form a human resource inventory to track what skills and capabilities need to be filled in to complete the human resources requirements.

When completed correctly, job descriptions can be a very important tool and can be used for many different functions, including:

- Giving employees a gauge of how they will be evaluated within the organization
- Helping determine the compensation level for individual positions
- Establishing hiring criteria for specific positions and giving candidates responsibility expectations

The following is a typical outline of a job description:

JOB TITLE:
Specific title that would be included in an organizational chart.

OVERALL DESCRIPTION:
A brief description of the responsibilities an individual holding this position would have.

REPORTING TO:
List of person(s) to whom this position reports, and any subordinate positions.

DUTIES:
A detailed list of regular duties this position would be expected to perform.

REQUIREMENTS:

A list of mandatory or preferred requirements for the position, including number of years of experience, certifications, and licenses.

CRITERIA:

A list of standards that will be used to evaluate the possible candidates, including specific skills, experience, or knowledge.

IMPLEMENTATION OF THE HUMAN RESOURCE PLAN

Once the planning part of the process is complete, the firm will set forth to implement that plan through the next set of human resource concepts and tactics: recruitment, selection, appraisal, rewards, and employee personal and professional development.

RECRUITMENT

Recruitment is the process by which companies attract candidates to fill present and future positions, and the appropriate method varies from company to company. In most cases, the human resource department in the company will work together with managers in departments throughout the company or with others familiar with the personnel needs to determine a recruitment method and approach.

Many recruitment methods are available, including Internet and print advertisements, employee referrals, and outsourced agencies (head hunters, executive placement firms, job placement agencies, etc.) that perform recruitment services for the company, either on a fixed-fee arrangement, much like a consulting relationship, or on a performance-based basis, where the fee is a percentage of the employee's salary. In some cases, the employee will pay the fees associated with such outsourced services, but more often, the company will pay these fees. Other recruitment tactics include job fairs and college recruiting and might involve a combination of several methods.

EMPLOYEE LEASING AND OUTSOURCING

In the past decade, the use of "employee leasing" and temporary, or project-based, outsourcing of human resource needs has become more prevalent. In this scenario, the company contracts with another company that provides the employees for a specific need or project. The contracted worker is an employee of the provider company, with the provider company responsible for payroll, employee taxes, benefits, and other employee-related expenses. The company hiring these contract employees is thus free of the associated bookkeeping and administrative costs of maintaining these employees on their payroll—it makes a single payment to the company from which they are leasing the employees, rather than paying the workers individually.

These leasing or outsourcing arrangements are attractive to new or emerging companies or to mature companies that may be experiencing an unusual spike in demand or some other kind of nonrecurring event, presenting a solution for a company that needs to modify its workforce capacity with some upside or downside flexibility.

RECRUITMENT: "INSIDE VS. OUTSIDE" THE COMPANY

One of the first questions the company's human resource department is likely to ask is whether to fill job needs internally or to look outside the company. Hiring internally allows the manager to choose from a known pool of talent and can minimize misperceptions among candidates about the actual requirements of the position. In addition, hiring from within can be cost effective and can provide motivation for existing employees.

Generally, it's advisable to look outside the company when specific skills are required for the position and existing employees may not be reasonably expected to train for or learn these skills. The decision to look outside the company tends to be more appropriate when there is a specific need to fill, such as technical requirements. Hiring from outside also helps to avoid the "ripple effect" of frequent internal staffing changes and the employee "musical chairs" syndrome that does not give staff time to mature into their respective jobs (though sometimes well-planned cross-training for different jobs within a company is a productive long-term strategy).

Finally, recruiting outside the company can be an effective way to import experience and creativity or new ways of doing things. This infusion of outsider perspectives and approaches can infuse the company with a fresh look at its processes and systems.

SELECTION

The recruitment process just described will result in a pool from which to select the "right" employee—and this usually involves a combination of different selection methods in order to make the best employee selection decision.

Interviews and reference checks are the most commonly used methods, but other methods are available depending on the specific demands of the position. For example, background checks are appropriate when a position requires that the employee have significant customer interaction or if the prospective employee has a fiduciary involvement or responsibility with the company. Other selection methods include:

- Skill performance tests/work samples—for example, a graphic artist may bring in a portfolio of past projects or a data entry candidate may be given a simulated work assignment to determine his or her relative efficiency.
- Drug tests—an increasingly used tool to select candidates without chemical or substance dependency.
- Personality tests—used especially in customer contact recruitment and selection (e.g., salespersons and customer service candidates).

- Physical abilities tests—used in many jobs where physical condition is an essential element in job productivity or success (e.g., a product-installation or delivery job).

INTERVIEWING

Face-to-face interviews can be extremely revealing but must be prepared for carefully. The goal of an interview should be to learn whether the candidate has the competencies and technical skills that are most critical to the job, and questions should be prepared for each area. The interviewer's questions should focus on behaviors, not opinions, and may involve asking applicants to provide examples from their past experience.

Interviews provide an opportunity to read body language and the applicants' ability to "think on their feet," often replicating the realities of life on the job. Additionally, to insure a good fit with the culture of the company, an initial interview is often followed up by several more representing the other employees with whom the potential hire may work if hired, as well as company representatives at different levels and areas within the company.

BACKGROUND AND REFERENCE CHECKS

When applicants are narrowed down to a few that look promising, it's time to get a look beyond just a completed job application and resume. Background and reference checks are a worthwhile investment of time and energy. Here are some rules for more effective reference checks:

- Ask the applicant to "bridge the gap" and inform prior employers that you intend to contact them. Former managers are much more likely to provide useful information if they are aware beforehand that they will be contacted.

- Open the call by describing the corporate culture of the organization. This provides some context for the previous employer's comments on the previous employee.
- Reassure the previous employers that the information they provide will not determine the final hiring decision but that your goal is to learn how best to manage the prospective hire.
- Save formal questions such as dates of employment and title until the end of the call.

EMPLOYEE TRAINING AND PROFESSIONAL DEVELOPMENT

It is one thing to be able to recruit and hire good employees, but to tap into and help them attain their full potential is just as—or even more—important. Training and development is an essential part of all organizations today. The main benefits of employee development and training include the following:

- Increases the value and capacity of the human assets of the company
- Provides an alternative to recruiting by having qualified personnel to fill vacant positions
- Creates potential future leaders of the company
- Helps reduce employee turnover by keeping individuals motivated and interested in their position with the possibility for advancement

ORIENTATION

Training should begin on day one of employment, with every employee given an orientation. Getting employees off to the right start is a very easy way to build a company that embraces learning and development. Most small companies do not have formal orientation programs but rely on individuals finding their way when they first get hired. This seems to work fine in smaller organizations where more informal means of communication are common, but as organizations grow, most find that formal orientation programs are necessary to get employees up to speed and productive in a timely fashion.

Formal orientation programs can range from an hour to several days, and the level of orientation usually depends on the level of the position of the new hire. Whereas entry level or unskilled labor will need very little orientation, experienced professionals will need quite a bit more to get up to speed with the organization. Each organization needs to define its own orientation needs and programs. Assigning mentors is often done in place of an orientation program to give new employees a helping hand during the first few weeks on the job. At a minimum, for small or large organizations, orientation programs should include the following:

- Detailed company history and overview of the current structure and products
- Overview of employment policies and handbook (if applicable)
- Basics of compensation, benefits, all other legal issues that arise
- Health and safety issues
- Information about business systems such as phone, e-mail, voice mail, and office equipment
- Employee rewards and incentives

SKILL TRAINING

Skill training provides training for employees in new skill sets. This could take many forms, including training on new software, accounting methods, customer service techniques, or even team-building exercises. Skill training has two main goals:

1. Maintain employees' current skill level with ever-advancing technology and business practices
2. Give employees the necessary skills to advance through the organization

Every organization has a unique set of skills required for its employees. Of course, many skills transfer from organization to organization very easily, but the scope of skills is usually unique for every organization. Prior to implementing training, organizations need to follow a few basic steps:

- Conduct complete skill assessments, involve all levels of employees, develop core skill competencies for each position, and assess current gaps in the skill set.
- Choose the training source. Whether you choose outside consultants, assign internal trainers, or devise online training, the source has to be effective for the given skill set.
- Align training with the broad goals and objectives of the organization. This will help employees see the importance and be more likely to jump on board with the training.
- Conduct training during work hours; this will help keep a positive attitude toward the training.
- Conduct training in suitable facilities. Sticking a class in a dirty warehouse is not likely to be very effective.
- Plan for feedback and assessment of all training programs.

PROFESSIONAL DEVELOPMENT AND LEADERSHIP TRAINING

As organizations grow, adapt, and mature, there comes a time when existing managers and leaders will begin to think about stepping down and looking for replacements either inside the organization or out. When this situation arises, very often managers find themselves unable to find qualified candidates with the right experience who will be a "good fit" with the current organization.

Managers typically find that internal candidates are very good at their current jobs but may not have the breadth of experience it takes to manage multiple departments successfully. External candidates may also be very experienced, but the "right fit" can be very hard to find. One way to ensure that suitable replacements for top managers and leaders are available is to have a program or plan to develop leaders internally.

Leadership development programs are very common in today's business world; the risk of not planning for the succession of current leaders is too high for most organizations to bear. One common measurement tool used by organizations is to ask the question, "Would the organization be able to survive successfully if the CEO or head manager were the victim of a fatal accident?" If the answer to this question is no, it would be wise for management to address this issue.

Leadership development programs take many forms, but they all have similar goals of providing certain employees with the necessary skills and experience to fill the shoes of top management in the future. The programs can be formal or informal, usually span several years, and should be recurring and fully accepted within the organization. Leadership and development programs usually involve scheduled job rotations with increased responsibility with every step. High-potential individuals are usually hired into the programs, mentors are assigned, and their progress is measured regularly. Of course, every individual who enters the program is not guaranteed a top management position. All program participants will have to prove themselves and take a proactive approach to develop professionally, and the hope is that when the time comes for management succession, there will be qualified candidates for selection.

360-DEGREE ASSESSMENT

The 360-degree assessment is a commonly used tool in organizations; it is a way of giving and receiving feedback at all levels within the organization. Simply put, a 360-degree assessment is a system used to gather input on an individual employees' performance, not only from managers and supervisors but from coworkers and direct reports as well. More traditional feedback tools, in which only the direct manager provides feedback, can very easily lead to a one-sided and incomplete employee review. The 360-degree assessment is much more likely to provide an accurate review and assessment of an employee's performance.

Here's how it works: Typically, all employees are given the opportunity to rate and give comments on all employees they work with on a regular basis, including managers, peers, and subordinates. Each assessment includes several different categories for employee assessment—for example, leadership, performance management, communication, teamwork, integrity, quality, problem solving, vision, trust, adaptability, and reliability. Each organization will develop the assessment criteria based on what it feels is important.

Once the assessment is complete, employees have the opportunity to view how their coworkers assessed their performance and managers get to see how their subordinates view them.

For instance, US-based computer manufacturer Dell has used 360-degree assessment, and the results have led to substantial management policy changes, including forcing upper management to be more in touch with the daily operations and allowing for routine opportunities for management to interact with subordinates.

Implementing the 360-degree assessment can sometimes be very difficult and can cause more harm than good if management is not careful. Giving feedback must be done with caution given the sensitive nature of the data and the possible defensiveness of the employees who receive it. Some employees will not be comfortable giving frank feedback to their peers. An organization needs to have a very high level of trust among the employees for this assessment to work effectively. If the level of trust is not established prior to the 360-degree evaluation, human tendencies such as protectiveness, revenge, and development of hierarchies will take precedence and will skew the results, creating even more distrust within the ranks. If this trust level cannot be established, the 360-degree evaluation should be postponed to a later date.

STEPS FOR IMPLEMENTATION OF 360-DEGREE EVALUATION

If a 360-degree evaluation has not been used previously in the organization, it might be wise to introduce the program as an internal program for personal improvement, not for management decisions. This will take the pressure off employees and allow for a more relaxed environment during the process. It may even be wise for upper management not to have access to the company-wide results the first time the assessment is given to help employees feel comfortable with the process.

Many large companies have the 360-degree assessment in place for more than a year before they are able to see any benefits from the program and use it to make decisions. Employees need to feel comfortable with the system before they will actually use it as a learning tool.

Start out with a test group

When first implementing the 360-degree evaluation, start out with one department or a small group of employees. The time and resources needed for a company-wide implementation can be substantial. Starting with a test group will provide insight on issues and problems that will arise and will limit the cost if the 360-degree evaluation does not work within the organization.

It's critical to link the 360-degree evaluation's goals with the overall company goals. The 360-degree evaluation needs full cooperation from all employees, along with a significant business reason for the implementation. If the program is linked to the overall goals, individual employees will have an easier time accepting and providing value.

Train employees

The 360-degree evaluation may include hiring an outside firm to handle the process, or if it is handled internally, there must be assigned roles and responsibilities. The employees who are responsible need to be trained on all aspects of the evaluation; they must ensure that complete trust is held throughout the process.

Turn the results into an action plan

Once the evaluation is complete, request ideas for an action plan from all employees' ideas. It's helpful to hold meetings if necessary or provide other means for feedback opportunities. Ongoing goals and objectives need to be set for the future in order for everyone involved to see that the program is effective and useful. Several questions should be answered prior to implementing a 360-degree evaluation program:

- How ready is the organization for the 360-degree evaluation?
- Who will be involved?
- Is this a mandatory or voluntary project?
- What criteria will be evaluated?
- How will the information be collected, compiled, and distributed?
- Who is going to be responsible for each activity, including planning, assessing, compiling the information, distributing the results, developing the action plan, and following through?

The 360-degree evaluation, if used correctly, can be a valuable organizational tool that will provide a path for personal and organizational development. It can help direct and mold the corporate culture, define and set goals, and create camaraderie among employees.

PERFORMANCE MANAGEMENT SYSTEMS

Since labor cost represents a major expense of the organization and, importantly, is often the main source of competitive advantage, it's also important to manage, evaluate, and seek areas to improve the organization's investment in human capital.

It's obvious that employers want employees who perform their jobs well. However, an effective performance management system increases the likelihood that such performance will occur. A performance management system consists of the processes used to identify, encourage, measure, evaluate, improve, and reward employee performance and seeks to link organizational strategy to results.

As identified by HR professionals, a performance management system should do the following:

- Provide information to employees about their performance
- Clarify what the organization expects
- Identify development needs
- Document performance for personal records

HUMAN RESOURCE MANAGEMENT AS A SOURCE OF COMPETITIVE ADVANTAGE

Human resource planning has evolved over time from a basic tool used by companies to identify personnel needs to an integral part of an organization's strategy for making the most of its "human capital."

Increasingly, companies are finding that the strategic management of human resources can actually be a source of competitive advantage. For example, one company that has clearly used its human resources as the key driver of its competitive advantage is Southwest Airlines.

In the airline industry, competitors are using essentially the same kind of ramp, maintenance, and aircraft, and they also utilize the same physical locations (airports), yet Southwest consistently outperforms its competition, using the very same hard assets as its competitors. The telltale variable explaining the difference in relative performance between Southwest and its less-profitable competitors is its focus on the human side of its business model. Southwest has focused a great deal of its energy upon developing a highly productive organizational culture by crafting a human resources strategy that has driven its sustainable competitive advantage.

Additionally, companies like Whole Foods, SAS Institute, and Men's Wearhouse proactively address personnel issues in order to keep their employees happy with their jobs. It has been proven time and again that when organizations take care of their employees, the employees will take care of the organization.

Men's Wearhouse, for example, has a corporate philosophy of uncovering untapped human capital in all of its employees. It operates under well-defined values and believes the employees *are* the organization. The company provides training for all levels and, as an added bonus, provides very low-interest loans to employees. As a result, Men's Wearhouse has reaped unprecedented growth of more than 30 percent annually in recent years in an industry that is very competitive with very low margins. The company also benefits from low-to-zero employee theft and does not use any devices to try to prevent employee theft.

The Men's Wearhouse model can be transferred to any industry. It starts with well-defined goals and values to make human capital a competitive advantage for the organization. In the Men's Wearhouse example, the company's goal was to develop every employee to his/her fullest potential. Then once the goals and values are decided on, the organization developed programs to make them attainable and a reality.

SUMMARY

Human resource planning, recruitment, and selection are the initial steps in effecting the company's strategy by maximizing its investment in human capital. Think of the recruitment and selection like a funnel, with the wide part of the funnel collecting a wide assortment of candidates and the selection process sorting the candidate pool into a smaller group of qualified candidates, both from the standpoint of the skills needed for the job and from the standpoint of their fit with the organizational culture of the company. Both kinds of "fit" are needed to effectively advance the company strategy via its human resource capabilities.

Chapter 2

ORGANIZATIONAL BEHAVIOR

An organization consists of individuals with different tasks attempting to accomplish a common purpose. This purpose is the creation and delivery of goods or services for their customers. Organizational behavior is the study of how individuals and groups perform together within an organization. It focuses on the best way to manage individuals, groups, organizations, and processes. Organizational behavior is an extensive topic and includes management, theories and practices of motivation, and the fundamentals of organizational structure and design.

From the smallest nonprofit to the largest multinational conglomerate, firms and organizations all have to deal with the concept of organizational behavior. Knowledge about their firm's organizational behavior can provide managers with a better understanding of how it attempts to accomplish its goals. This knowledge may also lead to ways in which a firm or organization can make its processes more effective and efficient, thus allowing the firm or organization to successfully adapt to changing circumstances.

MANAGEMENT

Management is a term that used to be focused on direction and control. Now it is more involved with support and facilitation and the evolving notion of the manager as "coach." In conjunction with this role as a supportive facilitator, managers are now focusing on efficiently and effectively utilizing the intellectual capital of an organization. Intellectual capital consists of the knowledge, expertise, and dedication of an organization's workforce. The management of intellectual capital is necessary in order to get the most out of an organization's material resources and achieve organizational goals.

In practice, managers accomplish organizational goals through the process of defining goals, organizing structures, motivating employees, and monitoring performance and outcomes. The manager directs and harnesses the power of his or her organizational behavior. In performing these processes, a manager often takes on several different roles. These roles were described by Henry Mintzberg and include interpersonal roles, informational roles, and decisional roles. Interpersonal roles are ways in which a manager works and communicates with others. Informational roles are ways in which a manager acquires processes and shares information. Decisional roles are how a manager uses information to make decisions, which involves identifying opportunities and problems and acting on them appropriately, allocating resources, handling conflicts, and negotiating.

In order to fill these roles effectively, managers use skills that allow them to translate knowledge into action. Robert Katz describes three different sets of skills managers use, including technical, human, and conceptual skills. Technical skills are used to perform a specialized task. They are learned both from experience and education, and they can involve using a specific type of technology or process. Human skills are used when working with others and include, among other things, basic communication skills, persuasive ability, and conflict resolution. Conceptual skills are used in analyzing and solving complex interrelated problems. They require having a good understanding of the organization as a whole and understanding how the interrelated parts work together—for example, a good understanding of an organization's behavioral attributes, its weaknesses, and actions needed to achieve its goals and objectives.

EMOTIONAL INTELLIGENCE AND THE MANAGER

Daniel Goleman defined an important aspect of human skills in his work on emotional intelligence. Emotional intelligence is tied closely to management effectiveness and ultimately organizational behavior; it suggests that a manager's performance may be influenced by several factors:

- Self-awareness—understanding your moods and emotions
- Self-regulation—thinking about your actions and controlling destructive ones
- Motivation—working hard to accomplish your goals
- Empathy—understanding the emotions of others
- Social Skills—developing good connections and relationships with others

Understanding emotional intelligence is especially important in light of changes in organizational structures, which have created firms with less hierarchy and closer peer contact.

MOTIVATION

Motivation is an important driver in an organization and is crucial to the management of intellectual capital. Motivation underlies what employees choose to do (quality and/or quantity), how much effort they will put into accomplishing the task, and how long they will work in order to accomplish it. Employees who are motivated will work more effectively and efficiently and shape an organization's behavior. A motivated workforce will have a strong effect on an organization's bottom line. Motivation is strongly tied to job satisfaction. Job satisfaction is how an individual feels about the tasks he or she is supposed to accomplish and may also be influenced by the physical and social nature of the workplace. The more satisfied employees are with their job, the more motivated they will be to do a job well.

There are several important studies relating to motivation. These include Abraham Maslow's Hierarchy of Needs; Frederick Herzberg's study of hygiene and motivational factors; Douglas McGregor's Theory X and Theory Y, Theory Z; Victor Vroom's Expectancy Theory; J. Stacy Adams' Equity Theory; and Reinforcement Theory.

MASLOW'S HIERARCHY OF NEEDS

In 1943, Abraham Maslow developed a theory about human motivation called the Hierarchy of Needs. This theory has been popular in the United States and describes human needs in five general categories. According to Maslow, once an individual has met his or her needs in one category, he or she is motivated to seek needs in the next higher level. Maslow's Hierarchy of Needs consists of the following general categories:

- Physiological needs—these are the first and lowest level of needs; they relate to the most basic needs for survival and include the need for food and shelter.
- Safety needs—the second level of needs involves an individual's need for security, protection, and safety in the physical and interpersonal events of daily life.
- Social needs—the third level of needs is associated with social behavior; it is based on an individual's desire to be accepted as part of a group and includes a desire for love and affection.
- Esteem needs—the fourth level of needs relates to an individual's need for respect, recognition, and prestige and involves a personal sense of competence.
- Self-actualization—this is the fifth and highest level of needs; needs of this level are associated with an individual's desire to reach his or

her full potential by growing and using his or her abilities to the fullest and most creative extent.

As individuals move higher in the corporate hierarchy, they may see higher order needs as being more important than those of lower orders. Needs may also vary based on career stage, organizational structure, and geographic location. The hierarchy of needs could also lack effective application in different cultural contexts. Certain cultures may value social needs over psychological and safety needs. In addition, the theory necessitates that a manager be able to identify and understand an employee's needs. This is not always easy and can lead to inaccurate assumptions. Taken in the proper context, however, recognizing the importance of needs is a useful method for conceptualizing factors of employee motivation and thus being able to direct an organization's behavior.

HERZBERG'S FACTORS

In the 1950s, Frederick Herzberg studied the characteristics of a job in order to determine which factors served to increase or decrease workers' satisfaction. His study identified two factors related to job satisfaction: hygiene factors and motivational factors.

Hygiene factors are those that must be maintained at adequate levels. They are related more to the environment in which an employee is working rather than the nature of the work itself. Important hygiene factors include organizational policies, quality of supervision, working conditions, relationships with peers and subordinates, status, job security, and salary. Adequate levels of these factors are necessary to prevent dissatisfaction; improving these factors beyond adequate levels, however, does not necessarily lead to an increase in job satisfaction.

A different set of factors, identified as motivational factors, is associated with having a direct effect on increasing job satisfaction. These factors include achievement, recognition, responsibility, growth, the work itself, and the opportunity for advancement.

Like Maslow's hierarchy of needs, Herzberg's factors must be tempered by sensitivity to individual and cultural differences and requires that managers identify what employees consider "adequate levels." Managers sometimes simplify both of these theories and inappropriately assume that they know what their employees need.

MCGREGOR'S THEORY X AND THEORY Y

Douglas McGregor's theories focus less on employee needs and more on the nature of managerial behavior. These theories are based on the assumption that a supervisor's perceptions of her employees will strongly influence the way in which he or she attempts to motivate his or her employees. McGregor created two theories based on his studies called Theory X and Theory Y.

In the case of Theory X, a supervisor assumes that his or her employees are adverse to work and will do everything they can to avoid it. Acting on this assumption, the supervisor will exert tight control over employees, monitor their work closely, and hesitantly delegate authority.

In the case of Theory Y, a supervisor assumes that contrary to Theory X, workers are willing to work and would be willing to accept increased responsibilities. In light of these assumptions, the supervisor will provide employees with more freedom and creativity in the workplace and will be more willing to delegate authority.

Managers will seek to motivate their employees based on their perceptions of the employees' interests. This theory brings to light the variation in practice that can exist depending on the assumptions that managers make about their employees.

THEORY Z

Theory Z emerged in the 1980s. It attempts to motivate workers by giving them more responsibility and making them feel more appreciated. It was developed, in part, in the light of Japanese management practices, which allowed for more worker participation in decision-making and provided for less specialized career paths.

EXPECTANCY THEORY

Developed by Victor Vroom, this concept assumes that the quality of employees' efforts is influenced by the outcomes they will receive for their efforts. They will be motivated to the degree that they feel that their efforts will result in an acceptable performance, that such performance will be rewarded, and that the value of the reward will be highly positive. In order for managers to practically apply the theories associated with expectancy theory, they need to define the desired behaviors clearly. Once this is accomplished, the manager should think about rewards that could serve as possible reinforcement and how these rewards will have different values for different individuals. Employees must then be informed about what must be done to receive these rewards, and managers need to provide feedback on employee performance. If a desired behavior is achieved, the reward must be given immediately.

EQUITY THEORY

Equity theory, a result of the work of J. Stacy Adams, states that when individuals determine whether or not the compensation they receive is fair compared to their coworkers, any perceived inequity will affect their motivation. This sense of inequity can either be felt as negative inequity, when an employee feels he or she has received less than others who performed the same task, or positive inequity, when a worker feels that he or she has received more than others who performed the same task.

Either type of inequity can motivate a worker to act in ways that restore the sense of equity. Examples of employee behavior may include not working as hard, asking for a raise, quitting, comparing himself or herself with a coworker, rationalizing that the inequity will only be temporary, or getting a coworker to accept more work. To limit a perceived sense of inequity, employees should be compensated to the degree that their efforts contribute to the firm. This theory, however, is difficult to implement given the differences of opinion that might arise between an employee and a supervisor regarding what constitutes equitable pay.

To apply this theory successfully, it is important to address the employee's perceptions. This can be accomplished first by recognizing and anticipating that inequities can and will exist. It is then important to communicate clear evaluations of any rewards given and an appraisal of the performance on which these rewards are based. There may also be comparison points that are appropriate to share.

REINFORCEMENT THEORY

A "carrot vs. stick" approach to motivational behavior, reinforcement theory is concerned with positive and negative reinforcement. It applies consequences to certain behaviors. The four basic reinforcement strategies include

- positive reinforcement;
- negative reinforcement;
- punishment; and
- extinction.

Positive reinforcement motivates workers by providing them with rewards for desirable behavior. To be effective, a reward must be delivered only if the desired behavior is displayed. It should also be delivered as quickly as possible after the desired behavior is exhibited. Negative reinforcement, on the other hand, involves withdrawing negative consequences to motivate the desired behavior. This method of reinforcement is sometimes called avoidance because its aim is to have the individual avoid the negative consequences by performing the desired behavior. Unlike positive and negative reinforcement, punishment is not designed to inspire positive behavior but to discourage negative behavior. Extinction is the withdrawal of reinforcing consequences for a desired behavior. Its intent is to eliminate undesirable behavior.

SUMMARY OF MOTIVATIONAL THEORIES

In shaping and directing an organization's behavior, the seven theories discussed previously provide some insight into the organization's behavior. Several conclusions can be drawn from these theories.

NEEDS

Employees have needs. In order to motivate employees, supervisors should attempt to understand the breadth of their employees' needs. This is not always an easy task and requires open and frequent communication between managers and employees. By structuring a job so that it meets these needs, a supervisor can increase an employee's motivation.

COMPENSATION

Compensation is an important part of motivation, with a goal to compensate employees according to the contribution the employee makes to the firm. Employees will be dissatisfied if they feel that they are getting less than they deserve. In order to decrease the likelihood of perceived inequities, a manager needs to be proactive and informative regarding reward structures.

REWARDS

Employees need to know that the goal they are working toward is achievable and that when they accomplish this goal they will be rewarded in an appropriate and timely manner.

MOTIVATION: FROM THEORY TO PRACTICE

The insights drawn from the discussion of motivational theory highlight the importance of assessing needs, compensation, and rewards when creating an organizational structure that will increase an employee's job satisfaction and motivation and direct organizational behavior; some of these actions include implementing an adequate compensation program, increasing job security, allowing for flexible work schedules, and establishing employee involvement programs.

ADEQUATE COMPENSATION PROGRAM

Before determining how compensation should be determined, it is necessary to align the compensation program with several elements of the business.

Business goals

A compensation plan should be developed in light of a firm's business goals. Employees should be compensated to the degree that their efforts help the business accomplish its goals.

Employee goals

A compensation plan should be clear in stating individual employee goals. Employees are motivated when they need to know what goals they will be expected to achieve.

Achievable goals

The goals that individual employees are expected to accomplish must be realistic and achievable. If employees feel that the goals associated with their positions are unreachable, they will not be motivated to work. If a supervisor can set reasonable goals and make the employee aware that numerous achievable bonuses will be given if these goals are achieved, the employee will be motivated.

Employee input

Employees will be more satisfied with their job if they are consulted about the compensation plan before it is put into effect.

An adequate compensation program, taking the above issues into account, will affect employee motivation; a compensation plan should give the highest relative raises to the individuals who achieve the highest levels of performance. This type of system is referred to as a merit-based pay system and bases pay on performance. This can be effectively implemented in conjunction with an incentive plan that rewards employees for achieving specific performance goals. These plans stand in contrast to a system that provides across-the-board pay raises. This type of system will not motivate workers to put extra effort into achieving set goals.

JOB SECURITY

Employees who feel they are in danger of losing their jobs may not show high work productivity. Worker satisfaction can, and providing job security may, increase productivity. One way firms can increase job security is by providing cross-training in other functions. This will give employees the versatility to accomplish new tasks if their current position changes or is no longer available.

FLEXIBLE WORK SCHEDULES

In today's time-pressed world, many employees view time away from work as an important factor that shapes their at-work motivation and on-the-job productivity. There are several methods for allowing flexible work schedules that can meet the needs of employees seeking greater home/work flexibility. One of the more common is a compressed workweek. This system lets an employee work the same number of hours over the course of fewer days. Instead of working five eight-hour days, an employee might work four ten-hour days. Other examples of flexible work schedules include job sharing, where two or more people share a certain work schedule.

EMPLOYEE INVOLVEMENT PROGRAMS

Employee involvement programs seek to motivate employees by increasing their responsibilities or getting them more involved in decision-making processes. There are several types of employee involvement programs, and the more basic of these include job enlargement, job rotation, and teamwork. More ambitious programs include open-book management and worker empowerment.

Job enlargement

Job enlargement is a direct way to increase job responsibility. It involves expanding a position and giving an employee a greater variety of tasks.

Job rotation

A job rotation program periodically reassigns employees to new positions. In addition to increasing employees' involvement in the firm and adjusting their responsibilities, job rotation can also improve employees' skill sets, thereby increasing their job security. In addition, it can also relieve the boredom in the workplace associated with doing the same job over a long period of time.

Teamwork

Teamwork can be used to improve organizational performance by putting individuals with different positions onto a team and setting them the task of achieving a specific goal. Teamwork serves to increase an employee's responsibilities and involvement in the firm. The best types of teams are self-directed. This provides the team with the authority to make decisions regarding planning and executing the project at hand.

OPEN-BOOK MANAGEMENT

Open-book management is a challenging but direct way of increasing employee involvement and responsibility. It involves allowing employees to see how their job performance affects key performance indicators that are important to the firm. In order to institute this program, a firm needs to make key indicators available to employees and educate them on how to interpret key performance measures. Employees also need to be empowered to make decisions related to their position and training and be given the opportunity to see how these decisions affect the rest of the firm. Open-book management also necessitates an adequate compensation program whereby compensation is tied to performance.

WORKER EMPOWERMENT

Worker empowerment attempts to increase employee job responsibility as well as employee involvement. It does this by giving employees more authority and involving them in the decision-making process. Employees who are empowered can often make better and more informed decisions than a manager who is not directly involved in the process. Participative management is similar to worker empowerment. Although it does not provide employees with direct decision-making power, it encourages managers to consult closely with them before making decisions. Another type of participatory management is management by objective. This approach allows employees to set their own goals and provides them with the freedom to decide how they can best achieve these goals.

MEASURING JOB SATISFACTION

How does a manager know that after gaining an understanding of the theories of motivation and applying different approaches to increase job satisfaction his or her efforts have been successful? In practice, a manager must draw conclusions on a daily basis from social observations and interactions in the workplace. Sometimes, however, it is a good idea to conduct a more formal survey. This can be accomplished through interviews, surveys, or focus groups that often only involve a specific group of employees. Two useful surveys are the Minnesota Satisfaction Questionnaire and the Job Descriptive Index. Both of these surveys address areas of employee satisfaction with respect to different aspects of an organization and provide managers with useful information. They cover work, working conditions, rewards, opportunities for advancement, and the quality of relationships with managers and coworkers.

ORGANIZATIONAL STRUCTURE

Whether it is the beginning stages of starting a business or looking for ways to improve an existing business, it is important to think about the firm's organizational structure. Examining organizational structure will help answer questions about the ways in which a firm conducts business. Who is responsible for accomplishing various tasks within the firm? How are these individuals grouped? Who manages these individuals or groups? How do they manage them?

In essence, the primary goal of an organizational structure is to coordinate and allocate a firm's resources so that the firm can carry out its plans and achieve its goals and objectives. The fundamentals of organizational structure revolve around the following factors:

Division of labor

The division of labor involves two steps: dividing work into separate tasks and assigning these tasks to workers. Managers answer the following two questions:

1. What are the different tasks carried out by your firm?
2. Who is responsible for accomplishing these tasks?

Departmentalization

Departmentalization is the process of grouping similar types of jobs together so that they can be accomplished more efficiently and effectively. There are five different ways to departmentalize business activities. Different types of departmentalization can exist to varying degrees within a business. What types of departmentalization exist within the firm? Could the firm be "departmentalized" differently? There are several ways to departmentalize an organization:

- *Function:* an example of functional departmentalization would be a firm that has a marketing and finance department. It involves grouping tasks based on the function that the organizational unit accomplishes within a firm.
- *Product:* a consumer electronics firm, which has separate departments for camera and MP3 players, is using product-based departmentalization. In this case, departments are based on the goods or services that an organizational unit sells or provides.
- *Process:* a manufacturing firm that includes separate departments for assembly and shipping is an example of a firm with process-based departmentalization. In this case, departmentalization revolves around the production process used by the organizational unit.
- *Customer:* a bank with separate departments for its business and individual customers is using customer-based departmentalization. Departmentalization is based on the type of customer served.
- *Geographic:* an example of a firm using geographic departmentalization is an automobile manufacturing company that has different departments for each country in which it sells cars. In this case, departmentalization is based on the geographic segmentation of organizational units.

Managerial hierarchy

Managerial hierarchy relates to the way in which management is layered. It usually includes three levels, upper or top management, middle management, and supervisory roles. The higher levels of management generally have fewer employees but more power.

Span of control

Span of control is closely related to managerial hierarchy. At each level of management within a firm, an individual is responsible for a different number of employees. Span of control relates to the number of employees that a manager directly supervises. Span of control is determined by a number of factors, including the type of activity, the location of the workers, a manager's ability to delegate tasks, the amount and nature of communication between the manager and the individuals he or she is supervising, and the skill level and motivation of the individuals being supervised.

Centralization vs. decentralization

Centralization is the degree to which formal authority is centralized within a unit or level of an organization. Decentralization is the process of actively shifting authority lower in a firm's hierarchical structure. This effectively gives more decision-making power and responsibility to those in supervisory roles. Centralization and decentralization have their benefits and costs. While centralization provides top-level managers with a better overview of operations and allows for tighter fiscal control, it can result in slower decision-making and limit innovation and motivation. Decentralization, on the other hand, can speed up decision-making and increase motivation and innovation, but this is done at the expense of a top manager's view of the firm and financial control.

MECHANISTIC AND ORGANIC ORGANIZATIONAL STRUCTURES

The five structural factors discussed above give rise to numerous organizational possibilities. Mechanistic and organic structures are two possibilities at opposite ends of the organizational spectrum. They give shape to the concept of the factors of organizational structure. A mechanistic organization is characterized by the following structural factors:

- Degree of work specialization is high.

- Departmentalization is rigid.
- Managerial hierarchy has many layers.
- The span of control is narrow.
- Decision-making is centralized.
- Chain of command is long.
- Organizational structure is very tall.

An organic organization is characterized by the following factors:

- Degree of work specialization is low.
- Departmentalization is loose.
- Managerial hierarchy has few layers.
- The span of control is wide.
- Decision-making is decentralized.
- Chain of command is short.
- Organizational structure is flat.

INFORMAL ORGANIZATIONS

A formal organizational structure, represented by an organizational chart or written job descriptions, is not the only structure that exists within an organization. Between different departments and levels of hierarchy, various informal organizations exist within an organizational structure. Informal organizations consist of a network of channels of communication based on informal relationships between individuals within a firm. These organizations are often based on friendships and social contacts. In addition to providing information and a sense of control over the work environment, they can also be a source of recognition and status. Informal organizations can be examined more closely through social network analysis. This process maps the social relationships between individuals within an organization. Once they are recognized and understood, informal organizations can be utilized within an existing organizational structure in order to increase communication and overall effectiveness and efficiency.

LINE AND STAFF ORGANIZATIONS

The factors related to organizational structures also help describe different positions for individuals within a firm. Two examples of this are line positions and staff positions. Organizational structures often involve the interrelation between these two types of positions.

Line positions are directly related to the production of goods and services. They are common in firms that involve production, manufacturing, or providing financial services.

Staff positions are supportive in nature, helping those in line positions and top management more effectively achieve the firm's goals and objectives. Staff positions provide services like legal, public relations, human resources, and technology support.

REENGINEERING

Reengineering involves the complete redesign of a firm's structures and processes. It is done in the hopes of increasing a firm's operational efficiency and effectiveness by controlling costs, improving quality, improving customer service, and increasing the speed at which business is conducted. Once a firm has examined the five factors of organizational structures, it can better understand where it can make changes to align its structure with the firm's goals and objectives.

HIGH-PERFORMANCE ORGANIZATIONS

The goal of the high-performance organization is to effectively and efficiently utilize intellectual capital. High-performance organizations focus on employee involvement, teamwork, organizational learning, total quality management, and integrated production techniques. Employee involvement is accomplished through worker empowerment or participative management. Teamwork is accomplished though self-directed groups. Organizational learning involves gathering, communicating, and storing organizational information in order to anticipate changes and challenges and make more informed decisions about the future. Total Quality Management focuses on high quality, continuous improvement, and customer satisfaction. Integrated production techniques implement flexibility in manufacturing and services and involve job design and information systems to more effectively and efficiently use the resources, knowledge, and techniques that a business uses to create goods or services. It stresses the use of just-in-time production and service systems and relies heavily on computers to assist, control, and integrate different organizational functions. Implementing integrated production techniques requires speeding up communication and decision-making within the organizational structure.

The process of transforming an organization into a high-performance organization begins by actively seeking to understand an organization's worksite problems and opportunities and its purpose, mission, strategy, and vision. These elements must be tied together into a new mission statement and vision for the firm that is aligned with the organization's core values. In order to be successful, this process requires the active involvement of individuals from various levels and groups within the organization. The broad level of participation will also insure a greater level of acceptance in the organization. Once these initial steps have been taken, the factors of employee involvement, teamwork, organizational learning, total quality management, and integrated production techniques can result in organizational, individual, and community benefits. The organization will be more effective in achieving its goals, job satisfaction and employee motivation will increase, and the organization will be better able to contribute to the community as a whole.

Although there are numerous benefits associated with high-performance organizations, establishing and maintaining them is a difficult task. One of the most daunting elements is successfully integrating employee involvement, teamwork, organizational learning, total quality management, and integrated production techniques. These are not separate functions; teamwork must contain elements of employee involvement, organizational learning, and total quality management. This can be especially challenging for managers who, in addition to their regular functions, are asked to implement these changes. Managers can experience many kinds of resistance. Employees may feel that the changes could put them out of a job. They may be resistant to participate in group decision-making or in team-based activities. Managers may also experience obstacles related to cultural differences regarding hierarchy and participation. In light of these challenges, some firms succeed in only implementing some of the elements associated with high-performance organizations.

Successfully creating a high-performance organization requires a high degree of cooperation and a strong level of commitment and acceptance from all employees. It is a challenging and difficult process, but it offers significant rewards throughout the organization.

METHODS OF CONTROL

Managers achieve organizational goals by managing intellectual capital in order to get the most out of organizational resources. An important part of this process is monitoring performance and outcomes. This can be done in several ways. Two of the more common ways that directly affect organizational behavior are output controls and process controls. Controls relate to setting standards, obtaining measurements of results related to these standards, and taking corrective actions when these standards are not met. Managers must be judicious in their use of controls so as not to overburden the organization.

OUTPUT CONTROLS

Output controls are about setting desired outcomes and allowing managers to decide how these outcomes can best be achieved. Output controls promote management creativity and flexibility. This type of control serves to separate methods from outcomes and subsequently decentralizes power by shifting it down the hierarchical structure.

PROCESS CONTROLS

Once effective methods have been determined for solving organizational problems, managers sometimes institutionalize them in order to prevent the problem from recurring. These types of controls are called process controls and are a way of regulating how specific tasks are conducted. Three types of process controls are policies, procedures, and rules, formalization and standardization, and total quality management controls.

POLICIES, PROCEDURES, AND RULES

These are often used in the absence of direct management control. Policies are general recommendations for conducting activities while procedures are a more focused set of guidelines. Rules are the strictest set of limits and establish what things should and should not be done.

FORMALIZATION AND STANDARDIZATION

Formalization involves creating a written set of policies, procedures, and rules that simplifies procedures in order to guide decision-making and behavior. Standardization is the degree to which the actions necessary to accomplish a task are limited. It attempts to make sure that when certain tasks are carried out they are carried out in a similar fashion.

CURRENT TRENDS IN ORGANIZATIONAL BEHAVIOR AND DESIGN

Modern organizational structures are currently undergoing changes in response to new trends in the global business environment.

One of the more prevalent trends is the increase in network organization, or a "virtual organization" that consists of a group of independent firms communicating via the latest advances in information technology. It can include suppliers, customers, and even competitors. These firms operate as an alliance in order to share skills, costs, and access to each other's markets in order to work together quickly and take advantage of business opportunities. These types of firms are characterized by technology, opportunism, trust, and a lack of borders. They assemble and disperse in response to business opportunities.

Another trend affecting organizational structures is the increase in large global mergers. By their very nature, these types of mergers necessitate that a firm reexamine its existing structure in light of its new position within the larger structure. In addition, management decisions designed to increase employee motivation must take into account the culture context in which they are made. Global mergers can also increase the use of virtual groups and the diversity of membership characteristics.

SUMMARY

Organizational behavior is the study of how individuals and groups perform together within an organization. It focuses on the best way to manage individuals, groups, organizations, and processes. This chapter has covered the basics of organizational behavior by defining the nature of managerial behavior, addressing the fundamental theories and practices of motivation, explaining the basics of organizational structure, and discussing some methods of control.

Chapter 3

LEADERSHIP AND TEAM BUILDING

What are the qualities of good leaders, and what makes them successful? Think of some of the greatest leaders of all time. What made them stand out from others? We may think of adjectives such as *heroic, charismatic,* and *strategic.* These are all leadership qualities, but what really makes for a strong and successful leader?

Successful leaders are able to influence others. They use their innate qualities to inspire a workforce, a team, or a nation to achieve goals. Leaders can see beyond themselves and beyond the task at hand to look at achieving long-term goals by utilizing their strengths combined with the strengths of others. Effective leaders are able to manage relationships with others and create positive outcomes.

Winston Churchill often comes to mind as one of the greatest leaders in history. He was a talented orator and politician, but what made Churchill a phenomenal leader was his ability to mobilize and strengthen the will of his people through his words and policies. Although his strategic actions were often criticized at the time for being impulsive, Churchill allowed his belief in democracy and his intolerance for fascism to dictate his wartime policies. It was not only his passion for the policies but his ability to carry out his plans that made him a successful leader.

Leadership, such as that demonstrated by Churchill, is about inspiring others and doing the right thing. Leaders make change happen, but their values remain steady and unchanging. Most leaders not only have a long-term perspective on goals, but they have innovative ways of achieving their goals.

World leaders and business leaders alike can create triumph from disasters. Leaders learn from failure and have a steadfastness of purpose that keeps them focused on a goal or objective in spite of near-term setbacks or adverse conditions. Leaders are flexible in their execution and will make mid-course corrections and iterative improvements—leaders "bend but don't break," and they inspire those around them to stretch and do their best to fulfill the organizational mission. Leaders are able to energize those around them in order to create desired results without compromising their ethical standards.

LEADERSHIP VS. MANAGEMENT

As a globally recognized thought leader of contemporary practice in management and leadership, Peter Drucker suggested "management is doing things right; leadership is doing the right things".

Although sometimes used synonymously, *leadership* and *management* can be quite different. Leaders may be managers, but not all managers are leaders. So just what are the differences?

While the manager tends to have his or her eyes on the bottom line, leaders are more often looking toward the horizon, trying to find new opportunities for growth and development. A manager is usually satisfied with the status quo, whereas the leader is often challenging it.

Leadership often involves reinventing the job; strong leaders create their role in an organization or in the world system. Managers are often responsible for executing the task at hand, not thinking of future goals. Managers are responsible for maintaining, but leaders look to innovate. Managers may involve employees in their activities, but often on a "need to know" basis. Leaders, on the other hand, work to inspire those around them by trying to help others gain personal growth and development from their activities and by turning weaknesses into strengths. Companies with "leader-managers" throughout the corporate hierarchy are the most successful.

MANAGEMENT STRUCTURE

Each company or organization has a structure. Many of them are hierarchical, with multiple levels of management. Each of these hierarchical groups has different management roles and responsibilities.

The CEO is often the person who decides how many levels there will be in the organization, and this decision is made based on his or her experience and by matching the span of control with the capabilities of management. If an organization has too many levels, the decision-making processes may be inhibited, and also managerial learning may be restricted. Upper management may be too far removed from those who are actually carrying out the tasks.

For this example, we will use a three-rung hierarchy. The top rung often consists of a CEO, president, and/or owner; there also may be vice presidents who answer to the CEO and president. Top-level management is responsible for strategic planning, creating long-range plans, and setting objectives for the company.

Below the highest level of managers, most organizations have middle managers, such as regional managers, divisional managers, or directors. Middle management is responsible for tactical planning. They focus mainly on specific operations, projects, products, and customer groups and devise methods for improving performance and implementing the strategic plans set forth by the upper-level managers.

Under the middle managers, there is the supervisory level of management, which often includes project managers and supervisors. The supervisory level is responsible for operational execution and may also be involved in operational planning. They assign non-managerial employees specific tasks and monitor performance. Supervisory management is engaged in an organization's day-to-day processes.

ORGANIZATIONAL STRUCTURE AND DESIGN

As the levels of management within an organization's hierarchy will vary, the groupings of the organization's activities will also vary. Organizational design is important because it divides the organization's labor, unites the organization's command, creates the structure authority and responsibility, and shows the span of control throughout the organization.

The CEO generally decides how the company will be grouped. Three types of hierarchical groupings are outlined below: divisional, functional, and matrix. There is also a nonhierarchical organizational design, the lateral design.

DIVISIONAL

The divisional hierarchy is also referred to as "multi-divisional." In this organizational structure, all activities relating to a set of customers, a product, or a set of products will be grouped together into one division.

The divisional structure is most effective when it is used by a large organization and is spread out geographically. It is also effective for an organization that has a wide array of products or service offerings.

The advantages of a divisional organizational design are that it improves decision-making within an organization, fixes accountability and performance, and increases and improves coordination among functions. The disadvantages of a divisional design are that it may be difficult to allocate sufficient staff support, the organization loses some economies of scale, and it can foster rivalries among divisions.

FUNCTIONAL

In a functional hierarchy, which is also referred to as a "unitary form," the organization is divided up by functions that are organized into departments. For example, a hotel company may have different departments such as marketing, corporate communications, accounting, quality assurance, and customer service.

The functional design works best for a small company that is geographically centralized and provides a limited number of goods and services. An organization has outgrown the functional structure when it begins to experience bottlenecks in the decision-making processes and has difficulty coordinating departmental efforts.

Some of the advantages of having a functional design are that it encourages the technical expertise of employees and it also reduces the duplication of activities. The disadvantages are that it can create narrow perspectives and activities can be difficult to coordinate.

MATRIX

The matrix structure combines both divisional and functional structures. The CEO of XYZ Corporation will oversee the vice president of global marketing and also the president of XYZ's French offices. The director of marketing in France will answer to both the president of XYZ France and the vice president of global marketing. The matrix design is often used in companies that have a strong global reach. Many traditional management practices may have to be modified if an organization decides to transform its structure to a matrix design.

The matrix design allows an organization to reinforce and broaden its technical excellence, facilitates the efficient use of company resources, and allows for a balance in conflicting organizational objectives. Some disadvantages of the matrix design are that it can lead to an increase in power conflicts, can cause confusion among employees who have two bosses, and can impede the decision-making process.

LATERAL

In this organizational structure, there is no hierarchy. In a laterally led organization, the leadership spreads out among the divisions instead of being directed from the top down. There is a CEO, and below him or her will be all the department heads from all divisions.

An example of a company that operates in this manner is W. L. Gore, a company based in Newark, Delaware, that manufactures many different types of plastic goods. Gore has a unique structure in which employees don't have titles beyond "associate," and technically no one is anyone else's boss. Employees are responsible for deciding who is to be hired and how much their coworkers will be compensated. Innovation at Gore is strongly encouraged.

THE ROLES OF MANAGERS

Management is often expressed as the process of achieving an organization's objectives through guiding development, maintenance, and allocating resources. The primary roles of managers are planning, organizing, leading, and controlling.

PLANNING

Planning is the process of determining a course of action for future conditions and events with the goal of achieving the company's objectives. Effective planning is necessary for any business or organization that wants to avoid costly mistakes. Four different types of planning are associated with management:

1. Strategic
2. Tactical
3. Operational
4. Contingency

Strategic planning involves creating long-range goals and determining the resources required for achieving these goals. Strategic planning is the most far-reaching level of planning and involves plans with time frames from between one and five years.

Essential to the notion of strategic planning is that it involves an assessment and consideration of the organization's external environment, and that the organization is adaptive to these outside, noncontrollable variables, adjusting and possibly redirecting its strategy to account for this changing environment.

A company's strategic planning objectives often make the difference between the organization's success and failure; there are several steps to successful strategic planning:

Defining a mission

This step involves translating the vision of the organization into a mission statement, or written intention of organizational goals. Often companies have broad mission statements that inform stakeholders of the company's reasons for being.

Here are a few examples of corporate mission statements:

The Walt Disney Company's objective is to be one of the world's leading producers and providers of entertainment and information, using its portfolio of brands to differentiate its content, services and consumer products. The Company's primary financial goals are to maximize earnings and cash flow, and to allocate capital profitably toward growth initiatives that will drive long-term shareholder value.

GE is committed to serve the communities where we do business, to provide our customers with innovative, high-quality products and services and to protect the health of our workers and our environment.

The Nike Mission: To bring inspiration to every athlete in the world.

While having a mission statement is important, it is even more important to live up to that mission statement. An organization's mission statement holds it accountable to investors, customers, and employers. A good example of a company that didn't live up to its mission statement is Enron, which had a corporate mission statement that mentioned various corporate values, one of which was "integrity."

Setting organizational objectives

Organizational objectives are more concrete than the mission statement; they define the organization's desired performance in areas such as customer service, profitability, and employee relations. Objectives are usually time-based and have a measurable element. For instance: XYZ Company's marketing objectives will be to capture 12 percent of the market in widgets by the end of fiscal year 2005. Let's look at some other examples of organizational objectives.

Reebok has an organizational objective in relation to human rights:

Standing up for human rights is a Reebok hallmark—as much a part of our corporate culture and identity as our products.

Marriott has organizational objectives for the organization's diversity:

Marriott International's commitment to diversity is absolute. It is the only way to attract, develop, and retain the very best talent available. It is the only way to forge the business relationships necessary to continue our dynamic growth. And it is the only way to meet our responsibilities to our associates, customers, partners, and stakeholders.

Creating strategies to differentiate the organization from its competitors
This is when the manager recognizes an organization's strengths and utilizes them in order to find the company's niche in the market.

Some retail clothing stores are known for their bargain prices, such as Old Navy; other retailers are known for their high-end products, such as Neiman Marcus. Nordstrom, the upscale Seattle-based retailer, differentiates itself with its level of customer service. Employees at Nordstrom are known for going above and beyond the ordinary in order to please a customer. The high level of customer satisfaction at Nordstrom increases customer loyalty and allows Nordstrom to differentiate itself from its competitors.

TAXONOMY OF PLANNING

Tactical planning denotes the implementation of the activities defined by the strategic plans. Generally, tactical planning involves shorter-range plans with time frames of less than one year.

Operational planning involves the creation of specific methods, standards, and procedures for different functional areas of an organization. In addition, the organization chooses specific work targets and assigns employees to teams in order to carry out plans.

Contingency planning involves the creation of an alternative course of action for unusual or crisis situations. In today's society, companies are stressing greater importance on contingency planning in order to respond to crisis situations. For example, realizing the impact of terrorism on businesses in the wake of September 11th, many companies have developed contingency plans to respond to potential terrorism events.

ORGANIZING

This management role involves blending human and capital resources in a formal structure. The manager will divide and classify work by determining which specific tasks need to be carried out in order to accomplish a set of objectives.

LEADING

Managers also have the role of leading or directing employees and plans. Some managers may be more successful at leadership than others. The goal of leading is to guide and motivate employees in order to accomplish organizational objectives. This role involves explaining procedures, issuing directives, and ensuring that any mistakes are corrected.

CONTROLLING

Controlling allows a manager to measure how closely an organization is adhering to its set goals. It is also a process that provides feedback for future planning.

Setting performance standards

A company needs to set the standards by which performance will be measured. In a sales organization, it may be sales growth or quarterly sales figures.

Perhaps the manager will set the dollar amount for sales that are to be made that quarter.

Measuring performance

Using the previous example, measuring performance for sales will require tallying up the number of sales made during the quarter.

Comparing actual performance to the set performance standards

Now the difference between the set performance sales and the dollar amount of actual sales made during the quarter must be determined.

Taking the necessary corrective action steps

If the sales were much below the set level, it is important to analyze what went wrong and try to correct it and use information from the process to set future performance standards.

LEADERSHIP STYLES

Individual managers have their own styles of managing, and within organizations there is often a predominant style of leadership. The predominant leadership styles—autocratic, democratic, and laissez-faire—have many variations. We can compare and contrast the effectiveness of each of these styles as it affects employee performance.

Autocratic leadership

This style of leadership is both directive and controlling. The leader will make all decisions without consulting employees and will also dictate employee roles. Micromanaging is a form of autocratic leadership in which upper management controls even the smallest tasks undertaken by subordinates.

The autocratic style of leadership limits employee freedom of expression and participation in the decision-making process. It may result in alienating employees from leadership and will not serve to create trust between managers and subordinates. Further, creative minds cannot flourish under autocratic leadership.

Autocratic leadership may best be used when companies are managing less-experienced employees. US companies operating in less-developed countries often use autocratic leadership. It allows the parent corporation more control over its overseas investment. In countries where the government controls the economy, US corporations will often use autocratic leadership because the employees are used to making decisions to satisfy the goals of the government, not the parent corporation.

Managers should not use the autocratic leadership style in operations where employees expect to voice their opinions. It also should not be used if employees begin expecting managers to make all the decisions for them, or if employees become fearful or resentful.

Democratic leadership

This style of management is centered on employee participation and involves decision-making by consensus and consultation. The leader will involve employees in the decision-making process, and they will be encouraged to give input and delegate assignments. Democratic leadership often leads to empowerment of employees because it gives them a sense of responsibility for the decisions made by management. This can also be a very effective form of management when employees offer a different perspective than the manager, due to their daily involvement with work. A successful leader will know when to be a teacher and when to be a student.

Democratic leadership may best be used when working with highly skilled and experienced employees. It is most useful for implementing organizational changes, resolving group problems, and when the leader is uncertain about which direction to take and therefore requires input from knowledgeable employees. One of the downsides of democratic leadership is that it may lead to endless meetings and therefore create frustration among employees if used for every decision made by a company. Democratic leadership is not a good idea in situations when the business cannot afford to make mistakes—for instance, when a company is facing a crisis situation such as bankruptcy.

Laissez-faire leadership

This free reign form of leadership, if it is to be successful, requires extensive communication by management with employees. It is the style of leadership that makes employees responsible for most of the decisions that are made, and in which they are minimally supervised. Employees are responsible for motivating and managing themselves on a daily basis under this leadership style.

Laissez-faire leadership may best be used when employees are educated, knowledgeable, and self-motivated. Employees must have the drive and ambition to achieve goals on their own for this style to be most effective. Laissez-faire leadership is not a good idea in situations where employees feel insecure about the manager's lack of availability or the manager is using the employees to cover for his or her inability to carry out his or her own work. This type of situation can create resentment and result in an unhealthy work environment.

As with many categories that describe business concepts, an organization and its leadership may apply any or all of these leadership styles. For instance, the managing partners of an architectural firm may utilize autocratic leadership style with the lower levels in its clerical and administrative functions but employ a democratic or laissez-faire leadership style with its professional staff of architect-associates and partners.

Two additional styles of leadership worth exploring are transformational and transactional. Both have strong ethical components and philosophical underpinnings.

TRANSFORMATIONAL LEADERSHIP

Leaders who have a clear vision and are able to articulate it effectively to others often characterize this style of leadership. Transformational leaders look beyond themselves in order to work for the greater good of everyone. This type of leader will bring others into the decision-making process and will allow those around him or her opportunity to learn and grow as individuals. Transformational leaders seek out different perspectives when trying to solve a problem and are able to instill pride into those who work under them. They spend time coaching their employees and learning from them as well.

TRANSACTIONAL LEADERSHIP

This leadership style is characterized by centralized control over employees. The transactional leader will control outcomes and strive for behavioral compliance. Employees under a transactional leader are motivated by the transactional leader's praise, reward, and promise. They may also be corrected by the leader's negative feedback, threats, or disciplinary action.

The most effective leadership style is using a combination of styles. Leaders should know when it is best to be autocratic and when to be democratic. They can also be transformational and transactional at the same time; these are not mutually exclusive styles and in fact can compliment one another extremely well.

LEADERSHIP AND MOTIVATION

An important role for a leader is motivating employees to do the best job possible. There are many ways a leader can motivate employees, and many of them do not require additional monetary compensation.

Sometimes motivation is brought about through creative means. Dallas-based retailer the Container Store offers its employees free yoga classes, a personalized online nutrition diary, and a free monthly chair massage. These techniques help relieve employee stress and make them feel appreciated. The company has consistently ranked near the top of Fortune's 100 Best Company Workplaces.

Open communication is also a key to motivating employees. When employees feel that they will be listened to and managers openly discuss matters with employees, a trusting relationship is created. At Harley-Davidson's headquarters, executives don't have doors on their offices, creating an open, trusting environment.

Another method to motivate is to ensure that employees are matched up with the right job. It is the leader's job to learn what employees' abilities and preferences are and match them to tasks that utilize their skills and, when possible, match with their preferences.

If a leader is a good role model, showing enthusiasm for his or her work and pride in the company, this will positively affect employee motivation.

At W. L. Gore, a salesperson's motivation comes from the approval of his or her peers. Compensation is based on rankings by the sales team members. Further, the company bases monetary rewards or bonuses on long-term growth and customer retention, unlike most companies that base bonuses on the bottom line. Gore also rewards employees who have performed "special achievements" during the quarter with a Proud Octopus Award trophy.

CORPORATE CULTURE

A corporate culture is the system of beliefs, goals, and values that an organization possesses. Many aspects of an organization influence the corporate culture, including workplace environments, communications networks, and managerial philosophies.

Strong cultures cause employees to march to the same beat and create high levels of employee motivation and loyalty. Corporate culture also provides control and structure to the company.

Having a strong corporate culture is not always the key to an organization's success. If the corporate culture is an obstacle to change, it can hinder a company's performance and ultimately its success. A misdirected culture can lead employees to strive for the wrong goals.

LEADERSHIP AND CULTURE

Leadership style is extremely important in an organization, as it often affects the organization's culture. Which style of management is right? It depends greatly on the type of organization and on the top management within the organization.

If managers are strong leaders, their style of leadership often predominates throughout the different levels of management within the organization. The leadership style is then responsible for creating the culture of the organization. There are good and bad hallmarks for leadership within an organization. If the corporate leadership style is deceptive, then often the management culture within the organization will be deceptive. The same holds true if the leadership is ethical.

It takes a strong leader to create a lasting culture within an organization. For ordinary leaders, it can take years to shape the attitudes and environment; only an extraordinary leader is capable of making revolutionary change.

CHARACTERISTICS OF SUCCESSFUL CORPORATE CULTURE

CARE

This involves employees taking responsibility for their actions and caring about both the customer and the good of the company. It creates high-quality customer service and a positive atmosphere in which to work.

CHALLENGE

If the CEO of a company states that employees should "think outside the box" but then squashes ideas because of their perceived chance of failure, this creates a contradictory environment. In this type of situation, a challenge to conventional thinking and performing causes employees to fear losing their jobs; creative employees will leave and a culture of "yes men" will be created.

RISK

A successful company will be able to manage risk and even turn it into a strategic and profitable advantage. It involves paying attention to reputation and earnings. Employees must anticipate the consequences of their decisions and actions. This type of risk management can add significant shareholder value.

ETHICS

Often ethics can be the glue that holds the culture of an organization together. An effective leader should create a written ethical code for the organization. This code of ethics should not only be enforced but continuously reinforced. The employee's ethics should serve as a standard by which performance is evaluated.

FOCUS

As Lewis Carroll famously noted: If you don't know where you are going, then any road will take you there. A leader has done his or her job well if managers have a sense of focus and continuity…if they know where the company or organization is heading. If managers feel that the direction of the organization is decided upon by which way the wind is blowing that day, rest assured that goals will not be met. It is important for employees to know where they are going and what they should be achieving, and it is the job of the leader to define this for them. The leader should always know where he or she is going at all times.

However, this does not mean that a leader should not be willing to change. In fact, a leader should be an agent for change, because stagnation does not often lead to success. It is important that while being accepting to change, a leader is able to align employees with goals.

TRUST

Mutual trust is an important hallmark of effective leadership. Management should trust the leader and the leader should trust management. It is important to note that micromanaging can kill the trusting culture. When employees come to trust one another, it creates a team environment, where everyone is working for the common goals of the organization.

MERIT

Organizations often meet their goals by rewarding employee performance based on merit. Merit systems create fairness and help to further foster a team environment.

INNOVATION

As globalization breaks down geographic limits, it's becoming critical to create a culture of innovation to bring new products, services, processes, and performance as drivers of long-term competitive advantage and sustainability. What is needed to bring innovation into an organization's culture?

- Formally adopt and support innovation by senior management and a core value for the organization.
- View innovation as a systemic process throughout the organization: all hands, all levels are involved in innovation.
- Provide resources, tools, and organizational support for innovation by all hands, all levels.
- Support a culture of innovation focused and fostered by trust among leadership and employees. In such a culture, employees understand

that their ideas are valued, trust that the organization gives them the right to express their ideas and oversee risk, collectively, along with the management.

- Reward innovation, not always financially, but always with recognition and validation.

LEADERSHIP TRENDS

COACHING

A new trend in effective leadership, coaching, has become extremely popular throughout different organizations. This style of leadership involves guiding employees in their decision-making process. When coaching, management provides employees with ideas, feedback, and consultation, but decisions will ultimately be left in the hands of the employees. Coaching prepares employees for the challenges they will face. The lower an employee's skill and experience level, the more coaching he or she will require. The interactions that an employee has with the manager are the best opportunities for enhancing his or her skills. Coaching enables employees to excel at their tasks. Instilling confidence in employees is extremely important. If management conveys the belief that employees will exceed expectations, it helps them do so.

A good coach will draw out the strengths of each employee and focus on how those strengths can be directed most effectively to achieve the organization's purpose and objectives. A good coach will also facilitate personal development and an improvement process through which the employee will be able to play a more effective role in achieving the organization's purpose and objectives. An effective coach also realizes that each employee is different, with different strengths and weaknesses, and that a coaching strategy must reflect this individualistic approach.

EMPLOYEE EMPOWERMENT

As organizations and companies become increasingly borderless, employee empowerment becomes ever more important. This trend in leadership has allowed employees to participate in the decision-making processes. Employee empowerment is also a method for building employee self-esteem. It also ties employees more closely to the company goals and will serve to increase their pride in their work and loyalty to the organization.

GLOBAL LEADERSHIP

As corporations become increasingly international in scope, there is a growing demand for global leaders. Although many of the qualities that make a successful domestic leader will make a successful global leader, the differences lie in the abilities of the leader to take on a global perspective. Global leaders are often entrepreneurial; they will have the ambition to take their ideas and strategies across borders. They will also have to develop cultural understanding; global leaders must be sensitive to the cultures of those working under them, no matter where they are based. Global leaders must also be adaptable; this is also part of accepting the cultural norms of different countries in which they are operating. They must know when to adapt the operational structure of the organization or adjust their leadership style in order to relate to those around them. However, as adaptable as they must be, global leaders should not adapt their ethics or values to suit local tastes. Global leaders must also serve as role models—fighting corruption, not giving into it.

EQUITABLE TREATMENT

An important trend in leadership is the equitable treatment of employees. This does not mean that each employee will be treated the same; it means that each employee will be given the amount of individual attention he or she requires, and it will involve leadership knowing his or her employees. A good leader will get to know employees well enough to give them what they need in order to best perform. For some employees, that may mean more structure, while for others it may mean more freedom. Some employees may need to be monitored more carefully, while others may work better independently. Leaders must know how to bring out the best in employees and how to build solid relationships with them; the most effective way of doing this is by getting to know them individually.

FEEDBACK

Employees thrive on feedback, and by providing feedback and communicating effectively, managers can give employees the tools they need to improve their performance.

Providing feedback will not dampen employee morale in most cases, but it will allow opportunities for employees to learn from their mistakes and perform their tasks better. Positive reinforcement should be used to encourage employees' positive behavior, but when criticism is necessary, make sure it is constructive. Managers can do this best by telling employees exactly what was observed and how they interpreted it; this also will allow employees to better understand what the manager saw in their performance and to explain if there has been a misunderstanding. This type of open dialogue between management and employees creates a more trusting atmosphere and is more likely to generate positive performance results.

PURSUING A LEADERSHIP ROLE

When pursuing a leadership role in an organization, it is important to gain insight into the elements of effective leadership.

FIRSTHAND EXPERIENCE

Drawing upon firsthand experience in leadership roles, good leaders think of the lessons learned from experiences, including experience in other organizational settings such as clubs or sports teams.

LEADER MEMOIRS

It is also important to read about other leaders. Most world leaders read books about leaders they admire. The books provide important insight into what it takes to be a leader and how to make decisions.

FIND A MENTOR

Learning from an accomplished leader is a great way to improve leadership abilities; it could be someone in the organization or community whose leadership is exemplary and who is willing to serve as a mentor; in fact, most leaders will probably be flattered and happy to help.

TEAM BUILDING

Teamwork is defined as a group of people working together to achieve a common goal. Team members are mutually responsible for reaching the goal toward which they are working. Team building is a process meant to improve the performance of the team, and it involves activities designed to foster communication and encourage cooperation. Additionally, the objective is to avoid potential disputes and problems and to keep the morale of team members high.

Many different industries and organizations use teams to accomplish goals, because people working together can often achieve more than they could individually.

How can you tell there's a need for a team to complete a project? Ask the following questions: Can this goal be attained individually? Can other people, or a team of other people, be more effective in achieving this goal? If the answers favor the involvement of others, it's time to consider forming a team.

In an increasingly complex environment, organizations are using a team approach to bring a diverse set of skills and perspectives into play. An effective use of teams often draws upon a creative approach of bringing together specialists that combine their efforts and develop intra-team synergies to meet the challenges of their often complex organizational environment.

An example of an industry that often uses teamwork is the construction industry. A successful construction project cannot take place without the formation of teams. A design team will be formed at the beginning of the project, and it includes architects, engineers, and project consultants. The design team alone, however, will not be able to complete the project. They will also need to form a team with the owner of the project and the contractor.

TYPES OF TEAMS

Throughout different organizations, there are different types of teams that are used to accomplish goals.

PROBLEM-SOLVING TEAMS

These teams are formed for a temporary period until a problem is solved, and then they disband. Team members often consist of one level of management. Let's say XYZ Corporation has lost 10 percent of its North American market share to MNO Widgets. XYZ wants to get this back by increasing sales across North America. All of XYZ's regional salespeople will be called in to form a team to regain that market share. Although their regional focus will remain, they will have to work together to solve the problem of regaining that market share, and when they achieve that goal, they will individually work on maintaining their hold in their market.

CROSS-FUNCTIONAL TEAMS

This type of team is made up of members from different areas of the business and often from a common managerial level. If a shampoo company wants to bring a new conditioner to market, a team will be formed and its members will consist of managers from different departments such as brand management, product development, market research, and finance. It is also likely that there will be involvement by marketing, communications, and design when the product comes closer to market.

STAGES OF TEAM DEVELOPMENT

FORMING THE TEAM

The first stage involves assembling the team and defining the goals, which should provide focus and be attainable. It is important that the team leadership understands the strengths of each of the team members in order to assemble a cohesive team. Often in the forming stage, team members will be extremely polite to one another; they will be feeling each other out.

An example of a goal that the team may set would be the project schedule. For a construction team, for example, certain stages of the project must be completed within a certain time frame to ensure that the project is completed on time for the owner. The design team designates the appropriate amount of time for each construction phase, and the builder will make a profit. It is important to agree upon and set this schedule from the beginning.

STORMING STAGE OF TEAM DEVELOPMENT

The second phase involves coordinating efforts and solving problems. If the teamwork starts to slip because of a difficult problem, it will be necessary for the team members to get the project back on track. Team members should be conscious of the team's health and whether or not the team is taking steps in the right direction to reach their goals.

Communication is extremely important to effective team performance in the storming stage. Effective teams communicate clearly and openly about problems. Ineffective communication can cause unnecessary tension and stress to team members. It is important that communication be relevant and responsive. Relevant communication is task-oriented and focused. Responsive communication involves the willingness of team members to gather information, to actively listen, and to build on the ideas and views of other team members.

ESTABLISHING TEAM NORMS

The project norms are an informal standard of conduct that guides the behavior of team members. This stage involves defining team roles, rights, and responsibilities. It is important to establish these norms at the beginning of the team-building process in order to avoid problems along the way. In addition to allocating responsibilities, it may also be necessary to allocate the risk that is to be undertaken by each team member. Each member of the team should have a sense of ownership of the project.

Allocating responsibility also means establishing a team leader. Team leadership should not be a top-down effort but should be more of a coaching role. The team leader must act as a cheerleader, encouraging each of the team members to work together, providing ideas, and serving as a role model.

There is often a period after the team has been formed when a conflict of personalities or ideas will arise. Team members begin to show their own styles; they are no longer worried about being polite. At this stage, there will be pessimism on the part of team members in relation to the project, and there may also be confusion.

TEAM PERFORMANCE STAGE

By this stage, the team is working together effectively, problems have been smoothed out, and achievements begin to become evident. A great deal of work will be accomplished at this stage. The team will be able to tackle new tasks easily and confidently. They will be comfortable using creative means. It is essential at this point to evaluate and report on progress that has been made.

PROJECT COMPLETION AND TEAM DISBANDING STAGE

The last phase of the project is completion. Often at this time, the team will evaluate the results, debrief, and take time to learn and improve its processes for use in future team-based projects.

SUMMARY

Leadership can greatly affect an organization, both by determining its success in the market and by defining the corporate culture. Strong, ethical leadership is extremely important in today's business climate. Although there are several different leadership styles, some of the most effective leaders are able to tailor their management practices to suit employee needs. Leadership is not only about being a great speaker or politician, it is about having a vision and being able to make that vision a reality.

Team building is another important aspect of business today. Many companies use teams to complete projects, and building an effective team is necessary to complete a project. Teams are most successful when they have a coach who is able to help see them through some of the more difficult stages of the team-building process.

Chapter 4

✿   ✿   ✿

ETHICS

Although ethics in business has been an issue for centuries, there are numerous recent examples of corporations and individuals who have run into legal and financial trouble due to their questionable ethics. Martha Stewart is an example of an individual whose ethics have been called into question. The accusation that she participated in insider trading, a violation of SEC regulations, brought her to court and made her the center of negatively charged media frenzy. While she was accused of committing the violation with her personal investments, the question of character cast a lingering shadow on her business. She stepped down from her role as CEO of her company, Martha Stewart Living Omnimedia, Inc., and K-Mart, which carried her brand-name products, brought a lawsuit against her. This was a clear situation in which ethical standards, whether of the individual representing the company or of the company itself, were tied to the company's bottom line.

An example of a company that committed serious ethical violations was Enron, the energy trading company. In fifteen years, Enron grew to be one of the largest companies in the United States, with more than twenty thousand employees in over forty countries. But by December 2001, it became clear that Enron was involved in a huge accounting scandal, the ramifications of which included the largest Chapter 11 bankruptcy filing in US history. Government hearings, at which several of Enron's top executives testified, were conducted to evaluate just how severe the wrongdoing was.

As a result of Enron's deceptive accounting practices, thousands of Enron employees lost their retirement savings, while several Enron executives received multimillion-dollar bonuses.

ETHICS: A DEFINITION

The definition of *ethics* is the moral standards used to judge right from wrong. In the business setting, ethics are the standards of moral values and conduct that govern decisions made and actions carried out in the work environment.

Unethical decisions are often made for the benefit of the decision-maker as opposed to the organization's stakeholders. Some examples of unethical behavior in business practice are

- saying things that you know not to be true;
- taking something that doesn't belong to you;
- buying influence; and
- hiding or divulging information.

CORPORATE GOVERNANCE

Often thought of as the system by which organizations are directed and controlled, corporate governance has come to take on more of an ethical slant over the past decade. According to World Bank former president James Wolfenson, "Corporate governance is about promoting corporate fairness, transparency and accountability."

CREATING AN ETHICAL STANDARD

Deciding what is right and what is wrong is not always clear-cut. The subjective nature of ethics creates the need for organizations to define their ethical standards. Company leaders often set the example for ethical standards. As discussed in the leadership chapter of this book, the job of the leader is to serve as a role model for employees. This is part of the reason why Martha Stewart's personal financial dealings were a concern to the company bearing her name.

Creating an ethical standard is an important way for a leader to spread his or her ethical beliefs throughout an organization. Often the ethical standards will cover a wide range of business areas.

INNER-ORGANIZATIONAL RELATIONS

An organization's ethics policies cover the areas of internal policies, which explain the company's responsibility to employees. These policies often include equal opportunities, sexual harassment, diversity, and employee safety.

Equal opportunity employment is protected by the Civil Rights Act of 1964, which prohibits employers from discriminating against prospective employees regardless of their race, religion, gender, or national origin. Today, employers include sexual preference as being protected by this act as well. Many companies have enacted policies of affirmative action in order to increase the employment opportunities for minorities and women within their organization. The Equal Employment Opportunity Commission (EEOC) enforces equal opportunity employment. Employees who feel their civil rights have been violated can file an official complaint with this organization.

Sexual harassment lawsuits have been much publicized over the last twenty years, and for that reason, many companies have enacted stringent policies and comprehensive employee training. These measures have been taken in order to increase employee awareness of what behaviors are not acceptable, as well as to make employees aware of their rights for dealing with sexual harassment by fellow employees.

Diversity in the workplace refers to the numbers of women and minorities employed by an organization. Many organizations hold diversity seminars in order to break down barriers and to increase cultural awareness and understanding among employees.

EXTERNAL ORGANIZATIONAL RELATIONS

Many organizations also create an ethical standard that covers issues concerning their effect on the outside world, including their responsibility to shareholders, customers, and the community.

One of the firm's responsibilities to shareholders is to make decisions with the best interests of the shareholders in mind. Many organizations encourage shareholder activism, which gives the shareholders the opportunity to influence management practices. As shareholders embrace ethical concerns, activism has also included influencing practices such as employee relations, social awareness, environmental practices, and other socially oriented concerns.

An organization has an obligation to its customers with regards to its production practices. Customers expect that a company will not produce a product or provide a service that has inherent defects or safety issues. Companies also will establish a standard for sales practices that discourages deceptive or aggressive sales methods, ensuring that employees understand what is acceptable and unacceptable behavior.

The social obligation that a company has can include environmentally sound practices. Environmental obligations include preventing air, water, and land pollution. A growing movement suggests that a company's social obligation also includes producing products that somehow benefit society or are not harmful.

THE IMPORTANCE OF WRITTEN STANDARDS FOR ETHICAL POLICIES

Many organizations opt for a written document that not only outlines the company's ethical policies but also follows government regulations. This document will then be distributed throughout the organization so that there can be no question of what the company policies are. This standard will often include guidelines for internal company behavior as well as for product quality and customer relations.

ETHICS TRAINING

With increasing frequency, companies are conducting ethics training sessions with employees. These training sessions involve the discussion and analysis of ethical dilemmas. Ethics training seminars are helpful in providing employees with the tools to make the right decisions in situations where their ethics are being tested.

CONSEQUENCES OF POOR ETHICAL DECISIONS

Enron illustrated how large-scale ethics violations caused the downfall of a company and legal entanglements for executives. Enron filed for Chapter 11 bankruptcy and sold off many of its holdings. Several executives were brought to trial. The ethics violations did not stop with Enron but spread to its accounting firm, Arthur Anderson, whose reputation was also irreparably tarnished for covering up Enron's accounting wrongdoings.

Despite the attention that has been given to ethics abuse by large corporations, smaller businesses suffer most from fraudulent activities, with research finding small business losses of up to 25 percent more than those of larger organizations due to fraud.

MONITORING COMPLAINTS AND ENCOURAGING FEEDBACK

Companies can deal with ethical violations by monitoring complaints and encouraging feedback. Complaints against the company by customers, shareholders, and employees should be monitored. Many companies also encourage feedback by providing toll-free telephone lines for customers to call or suggestion boxes for employees. This system of feedback makes customers, employees, and shareholders feel as though the executives are hearing their voices. According to research by the Association of Certified Fraud Examiners, organizations with hotlines set up can cut their losses from fraud by up to 50 percent.

GOVERNMENT REGULATIONS

As is the case when a social harm is identified, the federal government will step in and design regulations that will prevent further damage by unethical companies. Currently, the government protects consumers from unethical companies in several ways.

The Federal Trade Commission (FTC) monitors advertising to ensure that companies are not misleading the public with false advertising. The goal is to stamp out deceptive practices. Another government agency, the Food and Drug Administration (FDA), protects consumers by monitoring the safety and quality of many products. Additionally the government has many policies in place to encourage competition in the market, in order to ensure that consumers will not be charged unfair prices for goods and services in the market. To this end, the government's antitrust statutes prevent monopolies from forming. The government has also protected consumers from unfair pricing by deregulating industries, such as telecom, in order to allow more competition to enter the market.

WHISTLE-BLOWING

The most common detection method of occupational fraud is employee notice. While many employees choose to handle fraud accusations internally by reporting wrongdoings to executives, whistle-blowing is the employee's disclosure to the media or government of a company's unethical activities. Before employees step forward with information, there are several factors that they must consider:

- Can the ethical problems that a company is having be better handled internally?
- Is it worth staying with a company that does not value ethics?
- Does the unethical damage that has been done outweigh the risk of retaliation by the company?
- Can the whistle-blower risk the possibility of being harassed, disciplined, or fired, in spite of regulatory protection?

State and federal regulations exist to protect whistle-blowers. According to the Sarbanes-Oxley Act:

> *(e) Whoever knowingly, with the intent to retaliate, takes any action harmful to any person, including interference with the lawful employment or livelihood of any person, for providing to a law enforcement officer any truthful information relating to the commission or possible commission of any Federal offense, shall be fined under this title or imprisoned not more than 10 years, or both.*

ETHICS TODAY

Wrongful behavior has caused many citizens to take a skeptical view of large corporations. The managerial negligence that has been brought to light in recent years has caused global distrust of the US financial markets. The economic impact of these scandals, combined with distrust, has taken a financial toll on many in the US stock market.

As evident in the Sarbanes-Oxley Act, the US government endeavors to protect citizens against unethical corporations in addition to creating other new regulations, requiring more stringent accounting practices, encouraging an increase in transparency, and protecting those who step forward with information regarding corporate wrongdoings.

The cynical view of business ethics in the United States has caused organizations to go above and beyond what was done in the past to ensure that ethics are being enforced; for instance, corporations are creating positions for chief ethics officers.

But will these moves toward stringent ethical policies be enough to convince the world that US companies are ethical? The term *Enron Ethics* refers to the ironic difference between a company's outwardly ethical appearance and its internal ethical failure. From the outside, Enron appeared to be a model company, with its corporate social responsibility practices and thick book of ethical guidelines that was handed out to employees, while on the inside, the company was falling apart due to its faulty accounting practices. But Enron managed to pull the wool over the public's eyes for years. It's difficult for people to trust that other companies are not doing the same.

BEST PRACTICES

Some businesses stand out from others as far as their attempts at good corporate governance and business ethics are concerned.

GENERAL MILLS

At General Mills, the corporate culture is based on business ethics and corporate social responsibility. They are successful at being ethical because they follow their own standards and adhere to their core values. Employees are supplied with the company's written code of ethics and are expected to uphold the values of the corporation. The code of ethics reads:

- We strive for the highest quality in our products, services, and relationships.

- We set and maintain the highest standards for all aspects of our work.
- We advance and grow our businesses honestly and ethically, taking no shortcuts that might compromise our high standards.
- We comply with local laws in every nation where we operate. We recognize and respect the cultures, customs, and practices of our consumers and customers in nations around the world.
- We steer clear of conflicts of interest and work to avoid even the perception of conflict.
- We set very high expectations for ourselves—and for the integrity of our company. We will not compromise those standards.
- We deliver on our promises.
- We are ever mindful of the trust our consumers, customers, partners, and employees place in General Mills. We will never knowingly or willfully undermine that trust.

HEWLETT-PACKARD

Another company that has been recognized internationally for its outstanding corporate governance and ethics is Hewlett-Packard (HP), the computer and accessory manufacturer. HP has set high ethical standards to which employees are expected to adhere. Its core ethical values include:

- Honesty in communicating within the company and with our business partners, suppliers, and customers, while at the same time protecting the company's confidential information and trade secrets
- Excellence in our products and services, by striving to provide high-quality products and services to our customers
- Responsibility for our words and actions
- Compassion in our relationships with our employees and the communities affected by our business
- Citizenship in our observance of all the laws of any country in which we do business, respect for environmental concerns and our service to the community by improving and enriching community life

- Fairness to our fellow employees, stakeholders, business partners, customers, and suppliers through adherence to all applicable laws, regulations and policies, and a high standard of behavior
- Respect for our fellow employees, stakeholders, business partners, customers, and suppliers while showing willingness to solicit their opinions and value their feedback

CORPORATE SOCIAL RESPONSIBILITY AND CITIZENSHIP

Corporate social responsibility (CSR) can be defined as the concern of a business for society as a whole that goes beyond contractual or legal obligations. Many firms today are taking on CSR initiatives because, although it may not appear to help the company's bottom line in the short term, it often coincides with long-term sustainability and profitability. The subject of corporate obligation has been subtitled under numerous names, including key altruism, corporate citizenship, social obligation, and different monikers. As the terms imply, each carries with it a certain point of view on the part of business in society.

Corporate social responsibility is more than "being green"; it's a key factor in shaping strategy and long-term profitability, and it's turning into an indispensable part of brands' business methodologies.

The way brands approach corporate social obligation has developed from altruism to a genuine joining into business practices. Also, it is an inexorably paramount element customers consider when making buying decisions.

Nonetheless, some detractors dismiss CSR in an entrepreneur society where the essential obligation of business is seen as making money-related returns for its shareholders, and any activity that does not directly fiscally benefit an organization is regarded as a waste of corporate resources.

Given the gigantic movement toward CSR, the question for organizations is not whether to participate in CSR but rather what is the ideal path forward for making CSR programs that reflect an organization's business values and strategic objectives. CSR covers a wide range of issues, including but not limited to:

- unfair business practices;
- fair sales and pricing tactics
- producing products or delivering services that are not harmful
- complying with legal and regulatory matters
- safe, fair and respectful workplace environment
- fair and equitable employee compensation
- sensitivity to work/life balance and importance of family first policies such as family leave, child care, and employee wellness.

ENVIRONMENTAL IMPACT

Firms must ensure that their impact on the environment is at a minimum. This includes using environmentally sound manufacturing processes and producing products that do not damage the environment. Many companies have found that they can be successful financially while also being ecologically sound.

MARKETPLACE AND CONSUMER ISSUES

This involves ensuring consumer safety with the products that are produced and may involve monitoring and responding to consumer complaints. It may also involve ensuring fairness in the marketplace, giving consumers a choice and pricing products fairly.

COMMUNITY INVOLVEMENT

CSR also involves becoming active in the communities where the company operates. Activities may include funding local charitable organizations, sponsoring cultural events, or having volunteer days for employees to go into the community and participate in community service projects. An organization may also choose to create its own philanthropic arm, such as the Gap Corporation's Gap Foundation, which matches employee giving to philanthropic organizations.

Another term used frequently is *corporate citizenship,* the concept of companies holding to high ethical standards, environmental responsibility, providing safe and reliable products, and working to improve conditions in the community. Corporate citizenship encompasses business ethics, but it also has an element that goes above and beyond the legal and contractual obligations, similar to CSR.

A concept that is often referred to is the "triple bottom line." The basis is that companies should be working just as hard at increasing their social and environmental worth as they do to improve their financial results. The three lines are society, economy, and environment, and the lines are interdependent. But how can working hard at social and environmental worth benefit a company's bottom line financially?

BENEFITS OF GOOD CORPORATE CITIZENSHIP

According to the World Economic Forum's business case for corporate citizenship, there are eight areas where corporations can benefit from good governance and corporate citizenship:

- Reputation management—companies can avoid a damaged reputation by adhering to ethical practices.
- Risk profile and risk management—companies that adhere to more stringent policies (environmental, for example) are less likely to pose as much risk for investors because they are not taking chances with their reputations.
- Employee recruitment, motivation, and retention—companies that are better corporate citizens are more attractive to potential employees;

companies whose reputations are tarnished may have much difficulty recruiting new employees.

- Investor relations and access to capital—recent studies have shown that companies with sound environmental policies and environmentally safe products have been able to increase their earnings per share and are more likely to win contracts.

- Learning and innovation—adopting corporate citizenship principles can lead to creativity and employee innovation, because it requires finding solutions to problems while enhancing the company's bottom line.

- Competitiveness and market positioning—today consumers are very concerned about trusting companies and their products. Being a good corporate citizen will make a company more competitive and will help its position in the market.

- Operational efficiency—becoming more environmentally efficient often means reducing material use and waste, which enhances a company's bottom line.

- License to operate—companies that are good citizens are more likely to be given a second chance in case of a slip up than companies that have a negative image in the minds of citizens.

SUMMARY

Ethics and corporate social responsibility are very important topics in today's business environment. With the ethical downfall of Enron and others, some global investors are wary of investing in US markets. Companies must do their best to adhere to ethical standards. These ethical standards are a top-down effort from leadership. Ethics and good corporate governance lead to preference by lenders and investors. Organizations have found that being a good corporate citizen can benefit the company's bottom line while providing a halo effect if minor ethical infractions do occur. Companies are realizing that in order to achieve sustainability, they must become more socially aware and be more ethically conscious.

Chapter 5

NEGOTIATION

An executive's ability to negotiate skillfully is important because typically, whether they realize it or not, executives spend hours every week negotiating with subordinates, suppliers, lenders, significant others, children, parents, in-laws, car dealers, and others. Deciding how much to pay a new office manager or deciding where to go to lunch with a client involves negotiation. The office manager may choose to accept less money if 100 percent of health benefits are paid, while a client may agree to go for Mexican food if Chinese food will be the choice on the next occasion. Being a skillful negotiator requires patience, attentiveness, flexibility, and awareness of personal negotiation style, issues, and details of the case, as well as the goals and objectives of the other party.

Negotiation can be described as nonviolent communication between two or more parties who may have conflicting and common interests in an attempt to reach an agreement that meets the goals of one or both parties. In simple terms, negotiation is a process for getting something you want. As Gary Karrass, a noted authority on negotiation, once said, "We don't get what we want in this life, we get what we negotiate."

COMMON MISCONCEPTIONS ABOUT NEGOTIATION

Many people are afraid to negotiate because of all the stereotypes associated with negotiation. Although business owners spend up to half their time at work negotiating, many still feel uncomfortable with the process. Some fear that they may come across as impolite, pushy, unfair, or even cheap to the other party.

One common stereotype about negotiation is that good negotiators use tactics similar to the stereotypical deceitful, conniving used car salesman. Being a good negotiator does not mean you have to resort to being a slick, smooth talker.

Contrary to popular belief, negotiating should not be compared to a game or a war in which both parties enter the process with the goal of winning and crushing the other party's spirit. The end result of war or a game is that one party comes out as the clear winner and the other as the absolute loser. Upon completion of a successful negotiation, both parties should feel that they have won something.

Another reason business owners feel uncomfortable negotiating is because they feel they have to make trade-offs between getting along with the other side and getting what they want. It is not uncommon for business owners to feel that they have to give in to the other side's demands or play hardball in order to avoid conflict, damaging their future relationship, or being taken advantage of by the other party.

GENDER AND NEGOTIATION

Many people feel more relaxed when they find out that they will be negotiating with a woman because they assume that women are not as aggressive as their male counterparts and, therefore, cannot be as effective as negotiators.

This is another common misconception. While women tend to be more concerned with preserving relationships and men with arriving at an agreement as quickly as possible, this is not always the case. Some men are patient and are more interested in achieving a deal that meets the needs of all parties, while some women prefer to enter the negotiation with a competitive drive to win.

Whether you are negotiating with women or men, you should always do your homework. Learn as much as you can about the members of the other team, develop a relationship with them, and alter your negotiation style if necessary so that it resonates with the other team's personality.

PRIMARY GOAL OF NEGOTIATION

Negotiation is like neither a game nor a war. It is about cooperation and signing an agreement that makes both parties feel that they have been successful. The primary goal of effective negotiation should be to achieve a deal that both parties can live with and that accomplishes your goals without making the other party walk away from the deal or harming a valuable relationship. Basically, the whole point of negotiating with someone is to get something better than what you would get without negotiating.

NEGOTIATION STYLES

There are two main types of negotiation styles: hard and soft. Hard bargaining is also referred to as positional, aggressive, contending, or competitive bargaining; soft bargaining is synonymous with relational or cooperative bargaining.

HARD BARGAINERS

In a nutshell, hard bargainers want to be victorious and are willing to jeopardize relationships to accomplish their goal of winning. While this negotiation style eliminates the need to make concessions, it also increases the likelihood that the other party will walk away, resulting in no agreement, and that the relationship will be severed or severely damaged.

Hard bargainers consider satisfying the other party's needs only if it helps to accomplish their goals and objectives. They tend to withhold important information, purposely provide incorrect bottom line figures, and embellish facts. As a result of their sometimes-deceptive behavior, they tend to distrust the other party. Other traits displayed by hard bargainers are their inflated demands and threats, impatience, pressure tactics, and insistence on their position.

Because this approach involves little to no preparation, it is used by many negotiators. However, this negotiation style usually does not yield the best results because it alienates the opposing party and leaves them dissatisfied with the outcome. Before deciding to use this approach, serious consideration should be given to the following:

- How important is it that the other party does not walk away from the negotiation?
- How much do you value your relationship with the other party?
- How complicated are the issues?

If there's value to the relationship with the other side, it is important that the other party does not walk away from the negotiation, or if the matter involves complex issues, hard bargaining will most likely not yield the desired results.

SOFT BARGAINERS

In contrast to hard bargainers, the primary concern of soft bargainers is to maintain or improve relationships by finding a solution that appeases all parties. However, to avoid conflict with the other side, soft bargainers will quickly concede, make concessions, and agree to conditions that are clearly unfavorable for them. The major disadvantages of this approach are that soft bargainers often feel that they were taken advantage of or become bitter and resentful following a negotiation. Soft bargainers tend to be more patient, indirect, accommodating, and trusting than their hard bargaining counterparts.

So which negotiation style should be adopted? Hard or soft bargaining? According to Roger Fisher, director of the Harvard Negotiation Project, and William Ury, director of the Negotiation Network, the answer is neither. Fisher and Ury suggest a third negotiation style called principled or win-win negotiation. The main idea behind principled negotiation is that both sides explore the interests of both parties and discover a creative solution that makes both sides feel like winners. Fisher and Ury base principled negotiation on the following four points:

1. Focus on the interests of all parties, not their positions.
2. Separate the people from the issue.
3. Make a list of creative options that meet the interests of both parties.
4. Base the end result on an objective standard.

PRE-NEGOTIATION HOMEWORK

IDEAL MEETING LOCATION

If there's an established relationship with someone or there's been a previous negotiation history, negotiating over the telephone may feel comfortable to both parties. Otherwise, conducting the meeting in person is usually better than over the phone because it provides the opportunity to observe body language and to establish and maintain eye contact.

If it's agreed to meet in person, the party whose office is selected will have an advantage; it will be more comfortable for the party that is at "home," and securing approval from senior people, if necessary, can be done more quickly.

The main advantage of meeting at the other side's offices is to provide the opportunity to withhold information until there's a return to the "visitor's" office. Of course, if neither party is willing to agree to meet at "home" or "visitor," a natural solution is to meet at a neutral location.

SELF REFLECTION ABOUT NEGOTIATION STYLE

Before figuring out a way to improve a negotiation style, a negotiator needs to evaluate his or her current style and personality. Thinking about the last few negotiations, what tactics were successful and what areas could improve? What style was used (hard vs. soft bargaining techniques)? What were the hot buttons? The negotiator needs to think about how he or she reacted in different situations, and with such introspection and self-awareness the negotiator will be better prepared to handle himself or herself professionally while maintaining composure during negotiation activity. Such self-awareness can be an advantage when dealing with people whose tempers get the best of them.

ESTABLISH GOALS AND OBJECTIVES

To be a successful negotiator, it is imperative to engage in significant prenegotiation homework. Fisher and Ury suggest that half of the time allocated to the negotiation process be spent in preparation.

Fundamentally, the first thing to determine will be the primary goal and objectives—what the negotiator wants to achieve from the negotiation. The primary goal should be realistic and accessible. For example, consider the situation whereby the main goal is to hire a new office manager; it is unproductive to simply frame this vaguely as "the goal of the negotiation is to fill the office manager job vacancy." This objective needs further definition—for example, "hire a new office manager at a salary of $4,000 per month, with 75 percent of health and dental insurance paid by the company, ten days of vacation and five days of sick time for the first year, and match up to 3 percent of salary in the company's 401(k) plan."

RESEARCH THE OTHER TEAM'S MEMBERS AND PERSONALITIES

Once there's clarity about goals and objectives, the next step in preparing for negotiation is gathering information about the opposing party's personalities. If there's no previous relationship with the other side, begin to establish one by setting up a meeting or two prior to the negotiation. Perhaps you can meet informally over lunch one afternoon. If it's not possible to meet with the other side's counterparts prior to the negotiation, consider calling their assistants to find out more information about how to make them comfortable during the negotiation. Ask their assistants what they like to eat and drink so that you can have things prepared at the time of the negotiation.

Also, think about how to get their attention at the start of the negotiation meeting. What commonalities are there? Perhaps you share a common interest in an activity such as hiking, which would provide an opportunity to discuss trails and hiking experiences. If the representative of the other side likes to play tennis, ask about the last game he or she played or how well he or she played.

Does the other side use a hard or soft bargaining strategy? Can they be trusted? How long do they anticipate the process will take? Is it possible to find a disinterested third party who can provide information about them? What makes them tick? Are they impatient? Demanding? How long do they anticipate this process to take?

The more you can discover about the people on the other side, the more prepared you'll be for the negotiation, and this will also result in a higher degree of confidence during the entire negotiation process.

MAKE A LIST OF ASSUMPTIONS

Skilled negotiators realize that people sometimes mistake assumptions for what they believe to be facts. When negotiating with another party for the first time, we have to make certain assumptions as to what some of their expressions, phrases, or body language mean. Ask for clarification! Don't assume anything. Make a list of assumptions to bring to the negotiation and clarify any points that are unclear or uncertain.

GATHER FACTS AND CONDUCT RESEARCH

The next step involves gathering as much information about the subject of the negotiation. Let's say there's a pizza restaurant owner with an interest in negotiating prices with the landlord who owns the building where the pizzeria operates. To persuade the other side that the pizzeria owner is asking for something that is reasonable, the owner will need to provide supporting data.

For example, if the operator would like to renew the lease at the same price paid the previous year, the operator would need to prove why it would be unfair of the landlord to increase the rent. Research regarding real-estate prices in similar buildings located in the surrounding area of the restaurant, restaurant occupancy rates in the market area, the number of new restaurant openings in the past year in the market area, and the average increase in rent would be some topics worth researching prior to the negotiation. This type of information is available on the Internet, by asking for assistance at a local community library, by speaking with a local real-estate leasing agent, or by meeting with other building owners in the area. The pizza restaurant may wish to find out about what the current issues are in the real-estate industry. Another way to get the latest news and information regarding the real-estate industry is to read trade publications or visit the websites of real-estate trade associations for current articles.

FOCUS ON THE OTHER SIDE'S INTERESTS RATHER THAN STATED POSITIONS

It is important to find a win-win solution for both parties, to walk away from a negotiation knowing that both sides are satisfied with the results. If the other party is dissatisfied, it can have negative consequences. For example, if a customer feels he was cheated, an organization will lose the customer and perhaps future customers. If a new hire feels cheated out of a better salary, he or she may quit in a few months when something else comes along that pays more, after the organization has invested time and money in training. Leaving the other side feeling disgruntled, cheated, or deceived destroys relationships, which could be risky for business.

The next step in preparing for negotiation is to imagine the negotiation from the other side's perspective. Think about what it's like to be in their shoes and do their homework. What questions will they ask? Be prepared to answer them.

Although it seems like the most important question to ask the other side is what they want, Roger Fisher states that there is another question that looks at the underlying interests of the other party and is even more crucial. *Why do they want what they want?* Walk a mile in their shoes and determine what motivates their stated positions.

A well-worn parable illustrates how negotiation is about finding what's really important to the other side; the key "wins" for the other side may not be what seems obvious:

> *A coworker, Lisa, finds a bag of thirty oranges on sale at a local grocery store. She only needs ten of them, so she brings the remaining twenty oranges to the office to share with anyone who wants them. Both Karen and Anna decide they want them. After negotiating for a few minutes, they decide to each take home ten oranges.*

> *Karen wanted the oranges so she could squeeze fresh orange juice in her juicer. Anna wanted the oranges so she could grate the orange peels for an orange muffin recipe. If Karen and Anna had focused on their interests (one wants just the peels and the other wants only the juice) instead of their stated positions (wanting the oranges), they would have been able to share the twenty oranges and achieve their goals. Since neither side asked*

the opposing side why she *wanted the oranges, both Karen and Anna had to make a trip to the supermarket. Anna's recipe called for the rinds of twenty oranges and Karen needed enough juice for her family of five for breakfast, which also required the juice from twenty oranges. If they had focused on interests, they would not each have had to make a trip to the grocery store, and the peels of Karen's oranges and the orange juice from Anna's oranges would not have been wasted.*

Don't assume that every party's interests and motivations revolve around money. Let's look at a small marketing research firm looking for a new project manager. The owner has completed the interviews and is in the process of negotiating an offer with a prospective candidate. When the candidate is offered a salary of $50,000 a year, the candidate responds that the offer should be $55,000. When asked why the candidate thinks the job should pay $5,000 more than offered, the company owner realizes that money is not what is motivating the candidate. The candidate thinks the extra $5,000 should be offered in return for "settling" for the title of project manager, inasmuch as the candidate has ten years of project management experience and thinks the job should actually carry the title of project director instead of project manager. Further, the candidate is considering applying to an executive MBA evening program at the local university and feels a title of project director would be viewed more favorably by the university. Once the underlying motivation is discovered, the owner agrees to the title of project director and agrees to a salary of $50,000 a year.

Another example:

> *BOSS: Based on our conversations over the past few days, I would like to extend an offer to you for $44,000 a year plus ten days of vacation time and five sick days.*

> *EMPLOYEE: Well, I'm going to be honest and say that I am a bit surprised. I was expecting the offer to be closer to the $50,000 salary range.*

BOSS: Why were you expecting an offer of approximately $50,000?

EMPLOYEE: Well, since I have been freelancing for the past few years, I have grown accustomed to having more time to go on vacations. I work hard for most of the year, but I am also able to take a few weeks at a time to travel abroad. I will be unable to do much traveling if I have only two weeks of vacation time a year. So if I won't be able to travel as much, I should at least make more money.

BOSS: I see. How about this? I'll throw in an extra week of vacation for the next three years so you'll have fifteen days of vacation time. In addition to those fifteen days of vacation time, you will have five days of sick time. If you do not get sick during the year, you can use them as vacation days during the last quarter of the year. So if you stay well, you could have up to twenty vacation days your first three years! And if you work with me for three years, I'll increase that to twenty vacation days plus five sick days. And once a quarter, you can work ten hours either Monday through Thursday or Tuesday through Friday and take a long weekend off. I think that sounds fair. What do you think?

EMPLOYEE: I think I'll accept the offer. A salary of $44,000 sounds good as long as I have enough vacation time to travel.

BOSS: Great, welcome aboard then!

Upon first glance, it may appear that both parties want completely different things and have no interests in common. However, once it's uncovered as to what motivates the other side and their goals, it appears that both sides have more shared interests in common than opposing ones. Let's go back to the example about the small marketing research firm owner and the newly hired project director. The business owner and the new employee have a few interests in common. First, they both want the company to perform well. They both rely on the company's sales to support their families. Second, they both want stability. The owner wants the company to grow and would like to keep valuable employees. The company does not want to lose them to the competition, so the company offers them competitive salaries, vacation time, and benefits. The new project director is also looking for job security and doesn't want to have to switch jobs and move the family every few years to get a competitive salary and benefits. Third, both are interested in maintaining a good relationship with each other. The owner wants the employee to be happy with his or her job so that he or she stays around, and the project director wants to be able to use the owner as a reference or for networking possibilities in the future.

USE OBJECTIVE STANDARDS

In order to convince the other party that what is being asked for is fair and reasonable, use objective standards whenever possible. During the negotiation process with a prospective candidate, the employer will want to pay as little as possible and the employee will want to earn as much as possible. Rather than feeling the other party is being disingenuous and haggling back and forth, the easiest solution is to use an independent objective standard. Independent objective standards may include market value, replacement cost, depreciated book value, competitive prices, precedents for similar cases, scientific judgment, professional standards, moral or ethical standards, or government standards. Using objective standards can reduce the amount of time it takes to conclude a negotiation because they are more likely to be accepted by the other party as a fair and reasonable offer.

If the other party offers to pay or accept a specific amount, always ask how he or she arrived at that specific number. Did he or she use an objective standard? If so, which one? If not, suggest one be used in order to eliminate bias and be fair and create a win-win situation for both parties. If the other party is unable to provide details for how that amount was arrived at and refuses to budge, it may be just that the parties should agree to disagree and not negotiate. If, however, the price seems fair and is based on a trustworthy objective standard, be willing to be open-minded when confronted with a reasonable offer. Think about the following example:

DOCTOR: I am pleased to tell you that I met with everyone you interviewed with and would like to extend you an offer of $45,000 per year as your salary.

EMPLOYEE: How did you arrive at that amount exactly?

DOCTOR: Well, we think it is a very fair salary. According to our human resources department, the average salary paid to pediatric nurses with your level of experience in this city is $43,789. Not only do we pay slightly more than average, but we also offer other additional benefits. While most doctors offer their nurses two weeks of vacation, we would give you three. You would also be able to begin contributing to your 401(k) plan immediately rather than waiting for six months as is the case in many other offices. Additionally, the vast majority of our nurses have been with us for more than ten years. The average tenure at our office for nurses is fourteen and a half years. And every year for the past five, we have worked with a market research firm to conduct an employee satisfaction survey. According to last year's results, 92 percent of our employees are either satisfied or very satisfied with their jobs, 94 percent with the benefits, and 90 percent with their bosses. We really value our employees here, and I think they recognize that.

EMPLOYEE: Sounds like once nurses are hired at your office, they don't want to work anywhere else.

DOCTOR: Exactly. We have one of the highest retention rates in the city for nurses.

EMPLOYEE: Well, now that you have explained how happy your employees are, I think I would like to work here as well.

DOCTOR: I'm glad to hear it. I'll notify the human resources department and have them send your paperwork by the end of the day. You should receive it by the end of the week.

GENERATE A LIST OF CREATIVE OPTIONS THAT MEET THE INTERESTS OF BOTH PARTIES

Once you have figured out what the opposing party really wants, develop a list of creative options that meet the interests of both parties. Remember, if only one party's interests are presented, there's a risk of alienating the other party and, further, the possibility that they will lose their patience and walk away.

For an important negotiation, consider Fisher and Ury's suggestion of holding a brainstorming session with five to seven other colleagues off-site with a facilitator to generate a comprehensive list of ideas. Have the facilitator display the ideas on an easel or white board and record all ideas mentioned, unrealistic or not. Remind all participants that all ideas should provide a win-win solution for both sides. The unrealistic ideas can be tossed out when the group meets again before the negotiation to select the best ideas that will be discussed during the negotiation.

Make sure that all the ideas selected meet the following basic human needs that motivate the positions people choose so that you can reach mutual agreement more quickly:

- risk reduction and security—job security
- sense of belonging—fitting in at home and at work with specific roles and responsibilities
- economic security—being able to afford basic necessities (food, shelter, etc.)
- recognition and approval—feeling valued for accomplishing challenging work
- control over one's life—managing, organizing, and running one's life in the desired way

Consider this next example:

> *EMPLOYEE: Thank you for agreeing to meet with me to discuss my raise for next year.*
>
> *BOSS: I want you to know that I think you are an asset to my company and I appreciate everything you do around here. I think your review went well this year, and I have decided to give you an 8 percent raise for all your hard work.*
>
> *EMPLOYEE: I appreciate the 8 percent, but I have to say that I was hoping for 15 percent.*
>
> *BOSS: Please tell me why you were hoping for 15 percent.*
>
> *EMPLOYEE: Well, I really like my job, but it's expensive to keep my kids in daycare from 3:30 to 5:30 everyday. I was hoping for a 15 percent raise so that I can keep up with the rising costs of daycare.*
>
> *BOSS: I'll tell you what I can do. What about letting you work flexible hours? Maybe you could work from 6:30 a.m. to 3:00 p.m. each weekday, with a thirty-minute lunch. This way, you can still work forty hours a week and be home in time to take care of your kids when they come from school. Not only would you get to spend more quality time with your kids. If you have someone at home to get them ready for school then you may not have to send them to daycare.*
>
> *EMPLOYEE: Wow, that's a great idea. The 8 percent raise sounds fine. Thank you.*

The boss was able to meet his own needs of wanting to give his employee a raise of 8 percent and those of his employee by solving the daycare cost increase problems, leaving both parties feeling that they had won.

DETERMINE A BATNA AND THAT OF THE OTHER PARTY

In order to negotiate better, it's important to determine what the BATNA is prior to negotiating. BATNA, first coined by Fisher and Ury, stands for Best Alternative to a Negotiated Agreement. If the parties are unable to reach an agreement, what is the next best option? Knowing the BATNA helps decide at what point the deal the other side is offering you is no longer beneficial. Remember, the whole point of negotiating with someone is to get something better than what's possible without negotiating, so only consider sealing a deal if you are likely to come out ahead.

For example, let's take the case of the owner of a small advertising agency who's looking for a seasoned account executive for one of the agency's largest accounts. The owner is interested in a prospective candidate and is in the process of negotiating an offer. It may be helpful for the owner to generate a list of as many alternatives for not hiring this candidate and then pick the one option that seems to be the best.

Bear in mind there's a stronger position if the owner's BATNA is to hire a freelancer who used to be an employee of the agency until a permanent employee is hired. This person would require little to no training, since she is familiar with how the agency does things and would be able to produce work immediately. If, however, the owner has no other prospects in mind and would have to advertise the position to generate résumés and the official start date of the project is next week, the owner has a weaker BATNA.

Once the BATNA has been determined, consider the BATNA of the *other* party, keeping in mind that the party with the strongest BATNA tends to be the more powerful party in the negotiation process. In this example, if the prospective candidate has another job, the candidate has a more powerful BATNA than if the second best alternative is to remain unemployed for an indefinite amount of time until another suitable job is offered.

THE NEGOTIATION PROCESS

Once the negotiation process has started, the first thing to do after introductions is to make the other side feel at ease. If the meeting takes place in the office of one of the parties, make sure the "visitors" are comfortable with the temperature of the room, offer coffee, water, or something to eat if appropriate. Give the visitors a tour of the facilities so they know where the restrooms, phones, and computer access (if available) are in case they need to use them. Once everyone is comfortable, initiate small talk based on the research obtained via the "homework" stage of the negotiation process. Talk about any interests you may have in common, ask about their children, or discuss hobbies or any other interests they may have.

BE A GOOD LISTENER

Active listening skills are crucial to being a skilled negotiator. Being a good listener is challenging because of natural levels of stress during the negotiation. Additionally, listening requires concentration and patience. Although it's tempting to interrupt, be patient and concentrate on what is being said. Many people find it difficult to concentrate because they are too busy preparing what they will say next in reaction to what was said. With practice and prenegotiation rehearsing, the listening part of the negotiation session will be easier to achieve.

It's helpful to prove to the other side that their position and words are being paid due attention; this is an important signal to the other side and will engender a level of trust and, importantly, they will respond in a corresponding manner. To avoid having the other party feeling like everything they are saying is "going in one ear and out the other," it's helpful to appear genuinely interested and use physical gestures associated with paying attention, such as tilting the head and nodding.

Saying "Go on" or "I see" are other effective ways to show the other side they are being understood. Another way to let the other party know their communication is understood is by reiterating what has just been said in a succinct manner. Although actively listening to someone does not automatically mean agreement, make sure the other side knows their position is clearly understood. Acknowledging the other party's emotions helps them feel more comfortable so that both sides can move on to the problem-solving phase.

Listening to what someone is saying is a good start, but you must also pay attention to body language. Is the person avoiding eye contact or fidgeting? Does his or her body language seem trustworthy? Lee Miller, managing director of the Advanced Human Resources Groups, states that body language that suggests doubts include touching the nose, rubbing the ears, running fingers through the hair, or turning away from you.

If something that was said remains unclear or ambiguous, ask for clarification. And once something is mutually discussed, repeat it back in a succinct manner to make sure there are no misunderstandings.

ALTER THE NEGOTIATION STYLE, IF NECESSARY

There may be a need to alter a negotiation style, if necessary, to match the other team's personality. For example, if one side's approach is to be more indirect, but the other side gets right down to business once the meeting begins, perhaps there should be a change to be more direct. If the other side seems to be more analytical, include numbers, charts, and graphs to address the need to make the case in a way the other side would be more likely to understand.

SEPARATE PEOPLE FROM THE ISSUE

Fisher and Ury state that people become too emotionally involved with the issues of the negotiation and their side's positions. When the other side attacks their position or issues, they feel as if they are being attacked personally. It is important to separate the people on the other side from the issues. Instead of attacking the other party by saying, "Your company ripped me off!" explain the emotion of the opponent's action: "I felt let down."

Actively listening to the other side when they are speaking, acknowledging their emotions, and making a sincere effort to understand their point of view are ways to ensure there's separation of the people from the issues at hand. When people become emotional during a negotiation, it is important to recognize their emotions even if they seem outrageous or unreasonable. Simple phrases such as "I understand your frustration" suffice. Failure to notice their emotions may lead them to feel alienated or to an even stronger reaction.

BE CONFIDENT AND FIRM BUT NOT DEMANDING

One way to exude confidence during a negotiation is to practice, practice, practice. For example, work on listening skills the next time there's a "light" negotiation scenario—for instance, when taking a car to be repaired. We all negotiate every day with family, friends, and strangers, so there are ample opportunities to practice.

Another way to show control is by exhibiting positive body language. Lee suggests looking at others with direct eye contact, standing or sitting straight, smiling, projecting a moderate voice tone and pitch, and speaking slowly. Avoid phrases such as "I should have done more research in this area, but…" or "I'm not as experienced as the rest of you, but…" that may give the impression that you are unsure of what you are saying. Instead of asking the subordinated question "Can I have…" use the more assertive and confident "I'd like to have…"

BE PATIENT

It is important to remain calm and patient at all times, particularly when the other side is screaming, personally attacking, or behaving in an emotional manner. Although it may be difficult to maintain composure under tense circumstances, try to calm the other person down by acknowledging his or her emotional state and trying to understand the other person's point of view, followed by a brief fifteen-minute break. The person probably needs recognition, reassurance, security, esteem, or may just be having a bad day. The idea is to "kill them with kindness" and avoid bringing up this episode in the future to save face and embarrassment.

ASK QUESTIONS

Even with thorough preparation, there is no way to cover everything. Ask the other side questions to understand what their interests are and to clarify anything they may have mentioned earlier that may be unclear.

When asking questions to find out what the other party is thinking, be sure to ask open-ended questions, questions that must be answered with more than just a simple yes or no, inasmuch as these will provide more information from the other side. Open-ended questions tend to begin with words and phrases such as *who, what, when, why, where, describe a time when, please explain, please tell me,* and so on.

When the person has finished answering a question, refrain from immediately asking another question or making a statement. A few seconds of awkward silence is usually enough to make people uncomfortable, which influences them to continue speaking, and it may be possible to extract some more information from them.

DON'T BE AFRAID TO WALK AWAY

Sometimes, even though there's been dutiful homework, understanding of the other side's point of view and interests, and compilation of a list of creative solutions keeping the interests of both parties in mind, it may not be possible to reach an agreement with the other party. Although it is sometimes tempting to just sign a deal and get it done as quickly as possible and move on to other pressing tasks, be patient. If the offer on the table is worse than a BATNA, do not be afraid to walk away.

Sometimes when faced with abandonment, the other side will reconsider the agreement (but not always). Remember that what is being offered to the other side is valuable. Why else would the other party spend time trying to negotiate if it was not valuable to them? It may simply be the fact that another party will find the value and it's time to move on.

DIRTY NEGOTIATION TRICKS

There are several ways to undermine the negotiation process, so it's helpful to understand, and importantly, deal with "dirty tricks" that may be deployed by the other party.

NIBBLING

While principled negotiation is the ideal negotiation strategy, sometimes the other party claims to use principled negotiation but during the negotiation will begin using tricky negotiation tactics, which may range from using false data to lying. In this situation, call the other party on the dirty trick they are using, make a counteroffer, keep their interests in mind, and insist on using an objective standard. Although it may seem easier said than done, keep emotions under control when confronted with dirty tactics. Although it is human nature to respond under attack, something may be said that will be regretted later, and in many cases this is precisely what the other party is expecting to happen. Instead, smile, try to relax, and don't be intimidated.

After confronting the other party about their tricky behavior, continue with the negotiation process. Focus on the people, mutual interests, creative options, and objective standards. If unable to reach a fair agreement, evaluate the BATNA and consider walking away.

Let's look at the example of a florist shop whose owner negotiated a contract with a vendor for vases just three days ago. The owner is meeting today to sign the printed contract. When the meeting begins, the vendor says, "I know we agreed to all parts of this contract, but when I took it to my boss for approval, he told me that the company now requires payment in thirty days instead of forty-five." When one party "wants just a little bit more" toward the end of the negotiation, this is called *nibbling*. Until confronted with this behavior and called out, the other party will continue to do this.

The key when dealing with dirty tricks is to separate the people from the problem. In this example, the owner, instead of saying, "You tricked me! I'm not going to negotiate a deal with you liars," might try saying, "Well, as long as we're still in the negotiation process, there's one small thing we're not that happy about either. How about us paying you within thirty days of receiving a vase shipment if you will guarantee these prices through the end of June." The owner could also try saying, "Look, this agreement has already been approved by a lot of people from your side and my side. We have both already agreed that it is a fair contract, and I would prefer that we keep it the way it is."

GOOD GUY/BAD GUY

The good guy/bad guy routine, often seen on television shows and in movies about detectives and cops, involves two individuals. The bad guy is demanding, abrasive, and tough, while the good guy acts friendly, seems more anxious to make a deal, and appears to be almost embarrassed by his or her partner's harsh behavior. The good guy tries to befriend while the bad guy tries to intimidate. Although the two are working together, the good guy will try to work out a "deal" to avoid having to negotiate with the bad guy. The best way to handle this situation is to recognize the tactic and call it to their attention. "There seems to be some disagreement between you. Perhaps the two of you need a few minutes to sort out your objectives here today. Why don't we break for fifteen minutes while you work it out?"

ULTIMATUMS

This "take it or leave it" technique is usually designed to intimidate and quickly get a signed agreement. The best way to handle this technique is to ignore it and continue with the negotiation process that's more comfortable.

LIMITED AUTHORITY

A negotiation with someone who says he or she does not have the authority to agree or sign off on an issue is a limited authority dirty trick. Whether this technique is preplanned or legitimate, the appropriate response is, "I understand. Let's set up a meeting with the person who *does* have authority to negotiate on all the issues."

LATENESS/LONG INTERRUPTIONS

Waiting for someone to show up for a meeting or being stood up for a meeting is not only annoying but it is sometimes used as a dirty trick in negotiation. You find yourself wondering, "Am I on time? Were we supposed to meet earlier today and I wrote it down incorrectly in my calendar? Or maybe we were supposed to meet tomorrow?"

On other occasions, the other party arrives on time but is interrupted during the meeting and does not appear to have any interest in resuming the meeting. Consider someone who accepts a cell phone call in the middle of a negotiation and remains on the phone for more than thirty minutes while everyone else in the room waits for him or her to finish. These tactics are designed to make the other party feel intimidated and irritated. The antidote to this dirty trick is to announce: "You're obviously very distracted today, and I wouldn't want to take advantage of your inattention. Let's reschedule." This calls them out on this dirty trick while attacking the problem, not the people.

STATISTICAL DATA

If the other party has done its homework, they should be able to justify what they are asking for. However, pay attention to the source of their information. Just because the source is legitimate does not mean it is relevant. The Internet is an abundant source of information and misinformation to support multiple and divergently opposite positions. For example, let's go back to the case of the advertising agency located in Boise, Idaho. The owner is interviewing a recent college graduate for a position as junior copywriter. When the candidate is asked about salary range, the response reveals an expectation of $40,000 to $45,000. When the owner asks about the basis of that salary range, the candidate presents salary data found on a national salary survey website, but is not relevant to local labor market conditions such as those affecting Boise. The results have little bearing on getting a job in Boise, since they include national data instead of local data.

SUMMARY

Being a successful negotiator and using principled negotiation involves a lot of hard work and preparation. However, it can also be rewarding to walk out after a deal negotiation knowing that both sides got what they wanted. During the negotiation process, remember about uncovering the other side's motivating interests, a realistic determination of goals and objectives, and convincing the other party to use an objective standard. And if the other party uses dirty tactics, call them out, while being careful to attack the problem—not the people—and maintain composure and confidence and continue with the negotiation.

NEGOTIATION DOS

- Use good posture
- Speak slowly
- Smile
- Psyche yourself up
- Look the other party in the eye
- Be succinct
- Ask open-ended questions that must be answered with more than a yes or no
- Be a good listener—clarify, encourage, appreciate their efforts, recognize feelings, and summarize

- Think of creative solutions
- Ask for what you want
- Realize that you have something valuable
- Be willing to walk away
- Try to achieve a win-win negotiation
- Know what the other party wants
- Walk a mile in the other side's shoes
- Know your BATNA
- Determine the other side's hidden interests
- Ask for justifications and clarifications
- Ask questions
- Separate the people from the problem
- Use objective criteria
- Be flexible and open-minded
- Be credible—use facts and other supporting evidence
- Exude confidence
- Pay attention to your tone
- Make trade-offs
- Take notes
- Build relationships

NEGOTIATION "DON'TS"

- Make threats
- Fidget
- Interrupt when someone is speaking
- Shout
- Be sarcastic
- Criticize in front of others
- Attack people
- Insult or belittle
- Make the other feel guilty
- Pout

- Cry
- Call anyone names
- Be easily discouraged
- Beg
- Whine
- Take it personally
- Negotiate when you are feeling irritated, stressed, tired, or angry
- Use technical jargon
- Hog the floor
- Give ultimatums

Section II

MONEY: ECONOMICS, FINANCE, AND ACCOUNTING

Chapter 6

ACCOUNTING BASICS

A ccounting is the process of recording, classifying, reporting, and analyzing money. Accountants capture and record all the transactions, operations, and activities that have financial consequences for a business. Accountants are also involved in other activities in "finance" that impact a business, such as weighing the costs of new ventures, participating in strategies for mergers and acquisitions, quality management, tracking financial performance, as well as tax strategy.

While the accounting requirements of every business vary, all organizations need a way to keep track of the flow of money within an organization. The responsibilities of the finance and accounting functional area within an organization or by its chief financial officer (CFO) include:

- Facilitating operations—payroll, purchasing, cash collections, cash disbursements
- Management control—measuring actual performance against goals and expectations
- Management decision-making—analyzing cash position to make decisions

- External financial reports—financial statements prepared according to generally accepted accounting principles (GAAP) and available for audit
- Tax returns—federal and state income taxes, property, sales, and payroll taxes

Accounting and finance is not intuitive. Many small businesses hire accountants to set up and manage their books. Other companies use accounting software such as QuickBooks.

Accounting involves periodic reporting of financial data and includes:

- Business transactions. Businesses keep a daily record of transactions in sales journals, cash-receipt journals, or cash-disbursement journals.
- Debits and credits to a general ledger. An up-to-date general ledger shows current information about accounts payable, accounts receivable, owners' equity, and other accounts.
- Making adjustments to the general ledger. General-ledger adjustments let businesses account for items that aren't recorded in daily journals, such as bad debts and accrued interest or taxes. By adjusting entries, businesses can match revenues with expenses within each accounting period.
- Closing the books. After all revenues and expenses are accounted for, any net profit gets posted in the owners' equity account. Revenue and expense accounts are always brought to a zero balance before a new accounting cycle begins.

The first step in setting up an accounting system is deciding what to track, and that's where a *chart of accounts* comes into play. A chart of accounts is simply a list of categories of expenses, revenue, assets, and liabilities that is kept by an organization to record, sort, and review those accounting system entries. Whether it's a manual system or a software program, it's likely the organization will customize the chart of accounts to its particular business.

Account numbers are used as an easy account identification system. For most businesses, a three-number system will suffice; however, a four-number system is sometimes used for more complex ventures.

The chart of accounts is the foundation on which you will build an accounting system. Take care to correctly set up the chart of accounts the first time. Keep account descriptions as concise as possible, and leave plenty of room in a numbering system to add accounts in the future.

After setting up the chart of accounts, the next step is setting up a general ledger system, which is the engine that actually runs an accounting system on a daily basis.

CASH VERSUS ACCRUAL ACCOUNTING

The two principal methods of keeping track of the money that flows in and out of a business are cash and accrual accounting. Most small businesses use the cash method, in which income and expenses are tracked and summarized in accounting reports as they occur. Under the accrual method, the tracking may occur as incurred but the accounting records consider the timing of the benefit of revenues and the burden of expenses according to predetermined time periods where such revenues or expenses match up with each other.

ACCRUAL ACCOUNTING

In an organization using the accrual method, an accountant records income and expenses when they affect the organization, not when they actually receive or pay them. In practical terms, this difference in timing is relevant if your company keeps inventory on hand or handles transactions on credit. For example, a consultant completes a project in January but isn't paid for it at the time. The business that has been serviced recognizes all expenses in relation to that contract when they were incurred, regardless of whether the consultant has been paid or not. Both the income and expenses are recorded for the current tax year, even if payment is received and bills are paid the following February. The accrual method provides a better picture of the way revenues and expenses affect the financial condition of an organization and reflects "matching," an important tenet in accounting methods in which the costs and benefits of financial events are matched up in terms of timing the way they affect the organization's finances.

CASH ACCOUNTING

An organization using the cash method counts income when it is received and expenses when they are paid, irrespective of the timing of actual benefits to the organization. For instance, using the consulting firm example, the firm may not get paid for its work until the end of the consulting engagement, though the firm will incur expenses during the engagement. The expenses will be reflected in the cash method books in the months such expenses were paid for, though the revenue received when the project is completed will be reflected months later when that revenue is deposited into the consulting firm's bank account.

The cash method is usually associated with smaller organizations where it serves as a lower cost, less complicated, and basic approach for financial record keeping.

DOUBLE-ENTRY BOOKKEEPING

Without a system to record and track the flow of money within a firm, a business cannot accurately make clear operating decisions. In order to effectively operate, a business must ensure that the cash inflow from operating, financing, and investing activities is in balance with the cash outflows that are associated with expenditures.

To do this, accountants use a system of double-entry accounting to debit (remove) or credit (add) money as it flows in and out of their business. Double entry requires two entries per transaction, which provides cross checks and decreases errors. In the record of every financial transaction, the following equation remains in balance at all times:

ASSETS = LIABILITIES + OWNER'S EQUITY (CAPITAL)

Assets are what a company owns, such as equipment, buildings, and inventory. Claims on assets include liabilities and owners' equity. Liabilities are what a company owes, such as notes payable, trade accounts payable, and bonds. Owners' equity represents the claims of owners against the business.

The double-entry system provides checks and balances that ensure that the books are always kept in balance. Each transaction is recorded as a debit or a credit, with total assets equaling the sum total of liabilities and owners' equity.

DEBITS AND CREDITS

An understanding of debits and credits is essential in the effective usage of any accounting system. Every accounting entry in the general ledger contains both a debit and a credit. Further, all debits must equal all credits. If they don't, the double-entry system is out of balance. Therefore, the accounting system must have a mechanism to ensure that all entries balance. Indeed, most automated accounting systems won't allow an out-of-balance entry, they'll just beep until the error is fixed.

Depending on the type of accounting system, a debit or credit will either increase or decrease the account balance. For every increase in one account, there is an opposite (and equal) decrease in another. That's what keeps the entry in balance.

ASSETS AND LIABILITIES

Balance sheet accounts are the assets and liabilities for a firm. An asset is any item of value owned by a business. A firm's assets are listed on its balance sheet, where they are set off against its liabilities. Assets may include factories, land, inventories, vehicles, and other items. Some assets (short-term assets), like cash, are easy to value and liquidate, while others (long-term assets), such as buildings and farmland, are difficult to value and take longer to liquidate. These kinds of assets are collectively known as tangible assets.

Intangible assets, like a valued brand name such as BMW, don't show up on a balance sheet, but they do contribute to the value of the firm. There are many other intangible assets owned by a company. Patents, the exclusive right to use a trademark, and goodwill from the acquisition of another company are such intangible assets. Generally, the value of intangible assets is whatever both parties agree to when the assets are created. In the case of a patent, the value is often linked to its development costs.

Goodwill is the difference between the purchase price of a company and the value of the assets acquired (net of accumulated depreciation). Assets are those things of value that a company owns. Because a company has a right to the future collection of money, even something that is not physically in hand, such as accounts receivable, is an asset because a company has claim to money (an asset) due from a customer.

IDENTIFYING LIABILITIES

Liabilities are the opposite of assets. These are the obligations of one company to another. Accounts payable are liabilities that represent a company's future duty to pay a vendor. So is the loan from a bank. A business organizes liabilities into short-term and long-term categories on the balance sheet. Long-term debt (claims due in more than one year) and short-term debt (claims due within a year) are liabilities because they are claims against the business.

OWNERS' EQUITY

Owners' equity is the difference between assets and liabilities; it increases and decreases just like a liability. Owners' equity includes factors like partners' capital accounts, stock, and retained earnings. Stockholders' equity is also what would belong to the company's owners—the holders of its common stock—after selling the assets and paying off the creditors (providing the sales prices of the assets exceed the amount needed to pay off the creditors).

Retained earnings are the accumulated profits after dividends to common shareholders have been paid. At the end of one accounting year, all the income and expense accounts are compared to one another, and the difference (profit or loss for the year) is moved into the retained earnings account.

INCOME AND EXPENSES

Further into the chart of accounts come the income and expense accounts. Most companies want to keep track of where they get income and where it goes, and what's (hopefully) left over (profit).

INCOME ACCOUNTS

A business may want to establish an income account for different income-generating elements of a business. In that way, it can identify exactly where the income is coming from, and the income of the various sources can be added together. Examples of income accounts may include the following:

- Sales revenue
- Interest income
- Income from sale of assets

EXPENSE ACCOUNTS

Most companies have a separate account for each type of expense it incurs. A company probably incurs much the same expenses month after month; thus, once the company is established, the expense accounts won't vary much from month to month. Typical expense accounts include:

- Salaries and wages
- Telephone
- Utilities
- Repairs
- Maintenance
- Depreciation
- Amortization
- Interest
- Rent

THE GENERAL LEDGER

The core of a company's financial records is maintained in the "general ledger." These records constitute the central "books" of all financial transactions. The general ledger is integral for linkage to the company's financial reports.

The two primary financial reports of any company are the balance sheet and the profit and loss statement (income statement), and both are drawn directly from the company's general ledger. Every account that is on a chart of accounts will be included in a general ledger, which should be set up in the same order as the chart of accounts.

If a business is small and cash-based, the general ledger may simply be the company checkbook. The checkbook includes several pieces of information vital to the general ledger—cumulative cash balance, date of the entry, amount of the entry, and purpose of the entry.

An important element of a general ledger is source documents. Two examples of source documents are copies of invoices to customers and from suppliers. Source documents are critical in that they provide an audit trail to go back and study financial transactions made in a business. For instance, a customer might claim they never received an invoice from you. A source document will prove otherwise. Importantly, source documents are a required component for an accountant at tax time. Other examples of source documents include canceled checks, utility bills, payroll tax records, and loan statements.

All general ledger entries are double entries. This makes sense because for every financial transaction in a business, the money (or commitment to pay) goes from one place to another. For instance, when a payroll check is written, the money flows out of a payroll account (cash) into the hands of an employee (an expense). When goods are sold on account, a record of the sale (income) is generated, but there must also be a journal entry to make sure that the funds are collected from that account later (an account receivable).

COMPONENTS OF THE ACCOUNTING SYSTEM

Think of the accounting system as a wheel and the general ledger as the hub. Feeding the hub information are the spokes of the wheel. These include

- accounts receivable;
- accounts payable;
- order entry;
- inventory control;
- cost accounting;
- payroll; and
- fixed assets.

PAYROLL

Payroll accounting can be quite a challenge for any organization. There are many federal and state laws that regulate what must be tracked related to payroll. An organization may face fines for maintaining incomplete or nonconforming records. Many organizations will outsource payroll services, and by so doing guarantee their compliance with all applicable laws.

If payroll is maintained in-house, it is advised that an organization use an automated payroll system. Even if the books are done manually, an automated payroll system will save valuable time and help considerably with compliance.

ACCOUNTS PAYABLE

Accounts payable represent bills from suppliers for goods or services purchased on credit. Generally these obligations must be paid within twelve months. It is important to track accounts payable in a timely manner in order to know how much each supplier is owed and when payment is due. If an organization has a timely system in place to manage accounts payable, it may often be able to take advantage of discounts that are provided for timely payments. A poorly managed supplier system can damage a relationship with a supplier and earn a business a poor credit rating.

FIXED ASSETS

Fixed assets are commonly recognized as long-term holdings of an organization used in the production of its income. Fixed assets include real estate, facility, and equipment. Other types of assets include intangible fixed assets, which include patents, trademarks, and customer recognition. Fixed assets are items that are for long-term use, generally five years or more. They are not bought and sold in the normal course of business operation.

In an accrual system of accounting, fixed assets are not recorded when they are purchased, but rather their benefits to the organization are accounted for over a period of time that coincides with the useful life (the amount of time the asset is expected to last) of the item. This process is known as depreciation. Most businesses that own fixed assets keep subledgers for each asset category as well as for each depreciation schedule.

In most cases, depreciation is easy to compute. The cost of the asset is divided by its useful life. For instance, a piece of equipment worth fifty thousand dollars with a five-year useful life would be depreciated at a rate of ten thousand dollars per year. This is known as straight-line depreciation. There are other more complicated methods of fixed-asset depreciation that allow for accelerated depreciation on the front end, which is advantageous from a tax standpoint, and as such depreciation methods are considered, it is best to do so with the advice and involvement of a trusted tax advisor or a member of the organization's top management team who's leading its financial management function.

INVENTORY

For organizations producing things, a good inventory-control feature is an essential part of a bookkeeping system to track raw materials, work-in-process, and finished goods. Even a wholesaler or retailer will be selling many different types of inventory and will need an effective system to track each inventory item offered for sale.

Another key reason to track inventory very closely is the direct relationship to cost of goods sold. Because nearly all businesses that stock inventory are required to use the accrual method for accounting, good inventory records are a must for accurately tracking the material cost associated with each item sold. From a management standpoint, tracking inventory is also important. An effective and up-to-date inventory-control system will provide you with the following critical information:

- Which items sell well, and which items are slow moving
- When to order more raw materials or more items
- Where in the warehouse the inventory is stored when it comes time to ship it
- Number of days in the production process for each item
- Typical order of key customers
- Minimum inventory level needed to meet daily orders

ACCOUNTS RECEIVABLE

If goods or services are sold to customers with payment ("on account") expected in the future, the organization will need a method of tracking who owes how much and when it is due.

A good bookkeeping software system will provide the means to set up subledgers for each customer. Thus, when a sale is made on account it can be tracked by customer so that billing and collection are done in a timely manner.

ORGANIZING THE ACCOUNTING AND FINANCE DEPARTMENT

Many organizations organize the accounting system by function. In smaller organizations, there is often just one person in the office to do all the transaction entries. From an internal control standpoint, this isn't desirable because it opens the door for fraud and embezzlement. Companies with more people assigned to accounting functions don't pose as much of a threat for fraud perpetrated by a single person because the multi-person accounting department will provide for a means of checks and balances regarding financial transactions.

Having the same person draft the checks and reconcile the checking account is not a good example of how to assign accounting duties. Small businesses often can't afford the number of people needed for an adequate separation of duties; however, setting up a smart internal control structure within a new accounting system helps mitigate that risk.

ASSIGNMENT OF DUTIES

Most organizations need to cover the following accounting responsibilities:

- Overall responsibility for the accounting system
- Management of the computer system (if you're using one)
- Accounts receivable
- Accounts payable

- Order entry
- Cost accounting
- Monthly reporting
- Inventory control
- Payroll (even if the business uses an outside payroll service, someone must be in control and responsible)
- Internal accounting control
- Fixed assets

CREDIT CHECKING POTENTIAL CUSTOMERS

When an organization extends credit, it is in effect loaning customers money, and it wants to be reasonably sure the money will be paid back. The best assurance of being able to collect is to check each customer's credit history before extending credit.

However a business chooses to check a customer, it will want to build a credit relationship slowly and carefully; not every customer deserves the same credit terms, thus it's best to approach credit on a case-by-case basis. One thing to note is how long the company has been in business. Companies that have been around for at least five years are more likely to pay their bills on time—or they wouldn't be around anymore.

CREDIT REPORTS

It's always a good idea to obtain a potential customer's credit report before extending credit. Credit reports range in price from fifteen dollars for a one-page report to one thousand dollars for a detailed filing. The reports show historical payment data, bankruptcy records, any lawsuits, liens, and court judgments against a company, and a risk rating that predicts how likely customers are to pay their bills. Even if a prospective customer has little or no credit history, running a credit report is still worthwhile because it will reveal relevant data, including bankruptcy filings, corporate records, fictitious business name filings, court judgments, and tax liens.

CREDIT REFERENCES

In addition to credit reports, or for companies not covered by commercial credit reporting agencies, it may be possible to check a customer's credit references yourself. These references can be informative, but they aren't foolproof. After all, a customer picks his or her own references. To gain a more realistic picture, ask a customer for a comprehensive list of suppliers. Call several and ask if a potential customer owes them money. If so, find out if payments are being made in a timely manner. Ask for a list of other suppliers and other customers and contact them as references.

It may be helpful to call the customer's banker as well. While specific information may be inappropriate or illegal for a banker to provide, there may be some general information that's relevant. Ask how long the bank has had a relationship with the company. Has the bank given the company any credit? If a loan was given, did the company meet its obligations?

FINANCIAL STATEMENTS

A balance sheet can tell a lot about a company's ability to repay the money it borrows (but not necessarily about its willingness to pay—that would be reflected in a credit report). The ratio of the company's current assets to its current liabilities is an especially good indicator. If this number, called the current ratio, is less than one-to-one, the company is probably not a good credit risk. If the number is greater than two-to-one, extension of credit to this company is probably safe.

PERSONAL CREDIT REPORT OF THE OWNER OR CEO

When contemplating doing business with a new, closely held private company, it may not be possible to obtain a credit report, references, or financial statements. However, it's possible to run a personal credit check on the owner or CEO of the business. If that person has a strong credit history, it's likely he or she will see to it that the company pays its bills on time. If the owner or CEO has a history of debt dodging or late bill payment, the company might follow suit.

RED FLAGS

In addition to the standard inquiries into a company's credit situation, other things could indicate a credit problem: Does the business engage in unusual price-cutting or discounting strategies? Such practices may hinder the company's ability to pay what it owes in a timely fashion. Does the company already have trade credit relationships with other companies? Are any company assets already pledged as collateral? Does the company operate in a cyclical industry or in a business sector that is prone to seasonal turns? What is the general economic climate? When business is good it may be more appropriate to extend increasing amounts of credit. When things are slow, however, it's best to be more tight-fisted in extending credit to higher-risk customers. Finally, pay attention to the results of research. Sometimes no is the right answer when it comes to extending credit, no matter how attractive the potential revenue may be.

READING A CREDIT REPORT

A credit report is a snapshot of a company's or an individual's financial activities. Credit reports typically include historical payment data, bankruptcy records, Uniform Commercial Code (UCC) filings, bank loan information, leases, payment trends, and comparative industry data.

A typical credit report on a company contains its corporate name, address, and telephone number. It also includes the name of the chief executive officer, the company's Standard Industrial Classification (SIC) code, a description of its line of business, and the date when the company began operations. Also included are the number of employees, sales, and a net worth figure. In many cases, a report includes a numerical credit rating.

Financial information can run the gamut from basic sales and payment data to detailed transactional analysis. The information should include a summary of any lawsuits, liens, or court judgments that are outstanding, plus any relevant bankruptcy filings. If available, there will also be information on changes in ownership, relocations, company acquisitions, and publicly reported news events, including fires or natural disasters.

The amount of information depends on the stature of the company and whether it is publicly owned. Most credit report services focus on publicly held companies. Credit rating resources for privately held and newer companies are less formalized. To check payment practices for smaller companies, try talking to their customers, suppliers, and bankers.

Remember, too, that while credit reports can be important tools, they're not ends in themselves. Before making decisions based on credit reports, back up the information with data gleaned from other kinds of company research, as well as from customers, employees, and personal contacts.

GAAP ACCOUNTING RULES

Generally Accepted Accounting Principles (GAAP) is a set of nationally (United States) recognized accounting standards. Using GAAP accounting standards, costs and benefits are accounted for in a recognized way to assure consistency with firms' accounting principles and for comparing various projects and investments with one another.

PREVENTING OVERDUE ACCOUNTS

The best way to prevent overdue accounts is to avoid doing business with customers who have bad credit histories. However, doing business only with companies with a spotless credit record may result in a pool of potential customers that is quite small. And unfortunately, with a growing business, often there's no choice but to do business with a wider, and more risky, pool of potential customers.

The reality, especially in newer, fast-growing organizations, is that the business doesn't always have complete control of the terms of sales agreements; the biggest and best clients want to be billed quarterly and then have ninety days to pay, and their size and potential makes them significant and attractive.

On the other hand, there's a reluctance to destroy any potential or established business relationships by laying down harsh payment terms. Nonetheless, there's a need to take some control of accounts receivable to avoid negative results in cash flow.

The following steps can help cash flow without endangering it:

1. Watch for new customers with bad credit history—it's unlikely a company or a person with a history of bouncing checks or paying their bills late will change their ways. If needed, lay down credit rules early and firmly and start the relationship off slowly. Keep the amount of products or services to a minimum until the customer has proven itself worthy. And no matter how much the business is needed, never start doing business with another person or company until there's a signed contract clearly stating and agreeing to payment terms.
2. Once doing business with a customer on account, make sure to stamp invoices with the date that payment is due. Don't rely on the customer to look at the invoice date and, on their own, determine the pay date.
3. Offer discounts for early payment and add interest to late payments. A typical discount is 2 to 3 percent off the total if the bill is paid within ten days of the invoice date. The maximum amount of interest that can be charged varies by state.

4. Phone customers and start trying to collect soon after a payment is due. Never wait—let them know that your organization keeps close track of accounts receivable.

5. Until customers pay their bills, don't do any more business with them. Do not bend on this rule—it'll only cause more problems and scuttle any chance of collecting what's owed. If it's really important to keep doing business with an overdue customer, insist that any new products or services they receive from you are c.o.d. (cash on delivery).

COLLECTION AGENCIES

It's easy to extend too much credit when trying to entice companies into doing more business. Extending too much credit can lead to unpaid accounts, which can quickly and severely limit the cash to grow a business. If an organization doesn't stay on top of overdue accounts, the chance of collecting the money decreases over time.

One way to recover more from delinquent accounts is to hire a collection agency. A collection agency locates debtors and collects the money owed. If brought on board early, a collection agency can often recover a substantial portion of unpaid accounts.

In addition to increasing chances of actually getting paid, using an agency saves time and money—two extremely valuable resources. With their custom-designed phone systems, computers, and software, collection agencies are much more effective in recovering delinquent accounts.

Although collection agencies charge between 15 and 50 percent of what they recover, an organization will still end up with more than it probably could have collected on its own. When selecting an agency, think about the following considerations:

- Find out if the collection agency is a member of the American Collection Agency or the Commercial Law League of America, which require that their members adhere to a code of ethics and are familiar with the Fair Debt Collection Practices Act.
- Make sure the agency has insurance that will protect a business if the agency errs during the collections process.
- Ask the agency to disclose its typical recovery rate and provide a list of references. Contact some of the companies on the list and find out how long it took the agency to collect on late accounts, if they collected the whole debt or a portion of what was owed, and if they were satisfied with the agency's collection efforts.

SUMMARY

Organizations use accounting and bookkeeping methods and systems to "keep score" about financial health and performance; when these are diligently used, the organization can use these records as not only an evaluation tool, but also, when records are kept in a consistent manner, they can be used to manage the company from a financial perspective.

Chapter 7

FINANCIAL MANAGEMENT

The previous chapter covered accounting basics and the way an organization "keeps score" from a financial standpoint; this chapter dives further into how the information collected, organized, and reported for financial statements can be used to monitor, control, and fiscally manage the organization.

FIXED, VARIABLE, AND OPPORTUNITY COSTS

Fixed, variable, and opportunity costs describe different characteristics of costs borne by the organization in conducting its operation.

Fixed costs include all costs that do not vary with activity for an accounting period. Fixed costs are constant and unchanged regardless of the level of output or resources used. A fixed cost does not, in theory, vary with activity or sales. Such costs often include offices, factories, depreciation, and insurance or professional indemnity.

Variable costs are costs that vary as a function of an activity in running the organization. Variable costs include things such as sales commission (as sales increase, so do commissions paid to the sales force) or raw materials (as sales increase, so does the quantity of raw materials used to make the products being sold).

Opportunity costs refer to alternatives or opportunities that are sacrificed in favor of a chosen solution. Because resources are limited, any decision in favor of one project (service, goods, upgrade, etc.) means doing without something else. For example, an opportunity cost of opening an additional branch office in South Carolina may be the time and effort spent on the new branch that could otherwise have been spent on improving performance of existing operations.

ACTIVITY-BASED COSTING

A costing methodology associates specific efforts and personnel with specific tasks to gain a better understanding of how resources are being used. A simple activity-based costing examines work performed by a specific employee or work unit in a year and the cost associated with that unit's output. For example, a company considering outsourcing its payroll function may analyze how many people in the HR and accounting departments are involved in processing payroll each pay period, assess the salaries and overhead associated with those doing the payroll per pay period, multiply the number of pay periods per year, and arrive at an activity-based cost of "payroll processing." This assessment may then be compared to the quote from an outsource payroll preparation company to determine the relative cost/benefit of outsourcing versus internally processing the payroll function.

TAXES

Next to profits, taxes may be the most important issue facing every business, and while there's a responsibility to pay taxes, an organization will also be mindful to reduce the impact of taxes on its profitability. There are several tax-reduction strategies an organization may employ.

WRITING IT OFF: DEDUCTIONS

An organization can deduct all "ordinary and necessary" business expenses from revenues to reduce taxable income. Some deductions are obvious—expenditures in such areas as business travel, equipment, salaries, or rent. But the rules governing write-offs aren't always simple.

This area of the tax code trips up many an entrepreneur and is especially vexing for home-based businesses. Failure to keep up with an estimated tax bill can create cash-flow problems as well as the potential for punishing IRS penalties. The antidote is simple—know, and act upon, taxpayer responsibilities.

SALES TAXES

Many personal services (for example, hair styling) are under the taxable radar screen, but most products are taxable (typical exceptions are food and drugs). States keep adding to the list of taxable services, however, so check with a state's department of taxation to find out if you should charge sales tax on services. If you do sell a product or service that is subject to sales tax, you must register with the state's tax department. Then you must track taxable and nontaxable sales and include that information on a sales tax return.

LEGAL ENTITY FORM AND TAX IMPLICATIONS

The legal entity of an organization brings into play many considerations, and often it is the tax implication of one form of legal entity compared to other forms that guides the decision about what legal entity form to use.

For federal tax purposes, it's often best for a start-up company to be an S corporation or an LLC (Limited Liability Company) rather than a regular C corporation, though consulting with a capable tax professional is suggested to assist in making the best and most appropriate selection.

The important factor to choosing to be an S or C corporation or LLC instead of a sole proprietorship is the *limited liability* provided by a corporate entity. With limited liability, financial losses and the consequences of business failure are limited to the assets of the corporation and exclude the personal assets of those involved in the business. The protection afforded by this "corporate veil" is a cornerstone of business creation and is fundamental to formation of a strong economic system.

EMPLOYEE TAXES

A business is responsible for collecting and filing some taxes on behalf of its employees. The following is an overview of employee tax considerations.

GET AN EMPLOYER IDENTIFICATION NUMBER (EIN)

A business must report employment taxes or give tax statements to employees, and an Employer Identification Number (EIN) is needed to do this. Get Form SS-4 (application for Employer Identification Number) from the IRS website (IRS.gov) or by calling 1-800-Tax-Form (1-800-829-3676).

DEPOSIT EMPLOYEE WITHHOLDINGS ON TIME

Instead of paying the federal government directly, the employing organization makes a deposit with an authorized financial institution such as a commercial bank. Such deposits include: Employees' federal income tax (and state, if a state income tax is applicable) and both the employer and employee portion of Social Security and Medicare taxes.

ISSUE FORM 1099-MISC FOR INDEPENDENT CONTRACTORS

An organization may rely on independent contractors who pursue an independent trade in which they offer their services but are not employees. A worker is defined as an independent contractor if he or she controls the nature of his or her work and how it is performed. The Internal Revenue Service has a set of conditions that must be in effect to qualify for the status of an independent contractor.

AVOID PAYMENT PENALTIES

For an employer, paying and reporting employment taxes is a "fiduciary responsibility," and that responsibility is regarded very seriously by the IRS. It can impose deposit penalties ranging from 2 percent of the amount due (for payments that are one to five days late) to 15 percent (for amounts not paid within ten days after receiving the first IRS notice).

PREPARING FOR A TAX AUDIT

A tax audit is an experience every business hopes to avoid. If the IRS does pay a business a visit, however, understanding what an auditor might look for can make the difference between a minor inconvenience and a major hardship. During a full-fledged audit, an IRS agent may look at some or all of the following specific items in a tax return and business records.

Income

The IRS will compare bank statements and deposits to the income reported. They will also review invoices, sales records, and receipts, along with a general ledger and other formal bookkeeping records. They will also classify any exchange of goods or services in lieu of cash (such as barter transactions) as taxable income.

Expenses and deductions

An auditor may compare canceled checks, bills marked "paid," bank statements, credit card statements, receipts for payment or charitable gifts, and other business records to the expenses and deductions reported on a return.

They may pay special attention to reported debts or business losses; charitable gifts; and travel, meal, and entertainment expenses. Keep a log to substantiate travel, meal, and entertainment expenses and be sure to deduct only legitimate business expenses.

Loans and interest

An auditor may review loan paperwork, deposits, bank statements, credit card statements, and receipts and canceled checks to verify loans and interest deductions as business expenses.

Employee classifications

The IRS will review employee classifications on a return and check this data against time cards, job descriptions, benefit plans, invoices, canceled checks, contracts, and other business records. Auditors will pay particular attention to independent contractor classifications, because many firms improperly classify regular employees as contractors.

Payroll

Auditors will examine canceled checks, tax returns, deposits, business records, and other forms to check for completeness, accuracy, and timely filing. They will also review records documenting state, federal, and Social Security (FICA) withholding, Medicare taxes, advance earned-income credit, unemployment compensation, and workers' compensation premiums. The IRS will also examine salaries and bonuses paid to owners and officers of a business to be sure they are legitimate and within industry standards.

Other records

An auditor can also inspect records from a tax preparer or accountant, bank, or other financial institution; suppliers; and customers. In addition to inspecting a business, an auditor may inspect personal finances. The IRS may compare current lifestyle with the income presented on a tax return to determine if they are compatible.

Tax deductions

Taxes are an inevitable—and painful—part of every business. But there are ways to reduce, if not eliminate, a company's tax burden, if business-expense tax deductions are used to mitigate tax exposure. Common deductions include:

- Employee wages and most employee benefits
- Rent or lease payments
- Interest on business loans
- Real-estate taxes on business property
- State, local, and foreign income taxes assessed to a business
- Business insurance
- Advertising and promotion costs
- Employee education and training
- Education to maintain or improve required business skills
- Legal and professional fees
- Utilities
- Telephone costs
- Office repairs

A home-based business or a home office may also provide the ability to deduct a percentage of residential–real estate taxes, utilities, and telephone expenses. In addition, an auto, meals, travel, and entertainment expenses may be deductible if they relate directly to a business. As with all tax matters, it's best to seek the advice of a qualified advisor regarding the appropriate and generally accepted methods of tax and financial reporting for a privately held business.

Finally, always maintain complete and accurate business records to document deposits, income, expenses, and deductions. If the Internal Revenue Service audits a business, it may require evidence that each entry on a tax return is correct.

Chapter 8

ECONOMICS: LOCAL, NATIONAL, AND GLOBAL

E conomics is a social science that analyzes the choices made by people, organizations, and governments in allocating scarce resources. While this definition sounds rather theoretical, most people have a fairly intuitive understanding of the laws of supply and demand. When making purchasing decisions, we all decide what products or activities fit into our schedules, budgets, and needs and through these economic choices, we vote for what we want to be available in our market and at what price.

The economic system is the social institution through which goods and services are produced, distributed, and consumed. Economic decisions affect economic systems that are often global in scope. So today there is a combination of domestic and international factors that allocate resources and determine pricing of goods and services that we purchase and consume. These factors are in play at different levels and perspectives found in the study of economics: micro and macro economics.

MICROECONOMICS AND MACROECONOMICS

Microeconomics is the study of small economic units such as individual consumers, families, and businesses. It is the study of the individual parts of the economy that influence how prices are determined and how prices also determine the production, distribution, and use of goods and services. Macroeconomics refers to the study of a country's overall economic issues. Although these two different perspectives are often addressed separately, they are interrelated and together inform the way economic systems work.

A good example of how these areas cross over is with interest rates. Because of their ability to influence market activity, interest rates are a popular economic indicator. If interest rates are trending up, that usually means that the economy may also be considered to be active and moving upward. This relationship is referred to as *pro-cyclical* as it moves in the same direction as the economy and *coincident* as it moves along with the overall economy. If interest rates are trending down, that means that the economy may also be in decline.

Another perspective of economics is to consider the global implications of economic behavior and activity, especially when considering emerging economies such as in the Asian region with China, India, Indonesia, South Korea, Malaysia, Taiwan, and Thailand developing rapidly. In the Latin American region, Argentina, Brazil, Chile, Colombia, Mexico, Peru, and Venezuela are important. In the African region, Cote d'Ivoire, Ghana, Nigeria, Kenya, and South Africa are often economic focal points. In the European region, the Czech Republic, Greece, Hungary, Poland, Portugal, Russia, and Turkey are active in terms of their economic growth.

Irrespective of geographic location, the basic relationship of supply and demand is at the heart of economic activity, whereby supply is the willingness and ability of sellers to provide a varying amount of goods and services for sale according to a range of different prices. Demand frames the willingness of buyers to purchase goods and services at a varying range of prices. When buyers are willing to buy products or services at prices (demand) that align and are satisfactory to sellers, those sellers will produce enough of their product or service (supply) to match up with the buyers' demand. When these counterbalancing forces of supply and demand are in synch, the economic condition is referred to as being in *equilibrium.*

FACTORS DRIVING DEMAND

Another way to approach the study of economics is to consider how it focuses on the "wants" of the players in a market and the limited financial resources that they have to spend on their wants. The dynamics between supply and demand can be best understood when looking at a demand curve. The graph of a demand curve demonstrates the amount of product that buyers will "demand" (purchase) at different prices. They typically slope downward, meaning that demand rises as the price of a product falls and demand decreases as price rises. The sensitivity of the changes in price and demand is called price elasticity.

Products and services have different degrees of price elasticity. For example, if gasoline increases in price, overall demand may not be proportionately reduced, as people still need gas to fuel their vehicles (assuming there are no substitutes or alternatives—for example, a move toward using public transportation). If, however, the price of airline travel increases greatly, it may be likely that demand for air travel will have a greater-than-proportionate decline in demand inasmuch as it's relatively easy for travelers to seek other modes of transportation to satisfy their "want" to travel. This demonstrates a relatively high degree of price elasticity.

Businesses need to carefully monitor the factors that may affect demand. If they aren't keeping a careful eye on these different characteristics of demand, it can be assured that competitors will find a competitive advantage in better satisfying demand.

FACTORS DRIVING SUPPLY

The supply side of economics refers to the relationship between different prices and the quantities that sellers will offer: generally, if producers are able to garner a higher price, they will opt to produce more of that product or service.

ECONOMIC SYSTEMS

In the twentieth century, there were primarily two competing economic systems that provided answers to the questions of what to produce and for whom, given limited resources: *Planned Economies* directed by a centralized government and *Market Economies* based on private enterprise. History has proven that, worldwide, the central command-economy model has not sustained economic growth and has not provided long-term economic security for its citizens.

In fact, many government-controlled economies are turning to privatization to improve incentives and efficiency. Privatization is the selling of government-owned businesses to private investors. This trend has provided an opportunity for US firms to own businesses in foreign countries that previously prohibited US investment and, in many cases, entrepreneurially minded nationals secured rights and ownership in formerly government-owned enterprises in their home countries.

TAXONOMY OF COMPETITION

There are four different types of competition in a private enterprise system: pure competition, monopolistic competition, oligopolies, and monopolies.

PURE COMPETITION

Pure competition is an economic system with many competitors. It is easy to enter the market, as there are few barriers to entry and many people/organizations are able to offer products that are similar to each other. In a market where there is pure competition, a lower price becomes the key factor to buyers and their decision-making, and there is likely to be little differentiation between products. Additionally, the amount that each individual seller can offer constitutes such a small proportion of the overall market that when acting alone it is powerless to affect the price. Therefore, individual firms in these commodity-like markets have very little control over price.

MONOPOLISTIC COMPETITION

In this economic system, there are few competitors, but there is still competition. In this market environment, it is somewhat difficult to enter the market. The barriers to entry could be due to location, access to commodities, technology, or capital investment levels. The result is that there are usually differences in products offered by competing firms; perhaps they serve the same function, but there are differentiations that rely on consumer preferences to make a choice. Due to the differentiation factor, individual firms are able to have some sort of control over the prices. They can choose to charge a premium or a discount to set their product apart and affect the demand.

OLIGOPOLY

Oligopoly is a market situation also with few competitors. The few competitors exist due to high barriers to entry; thus, a few large sellers vie for, and collectively account for, a relatively large market share. Oligopolistic industries tend to be those that have a very high-level of capital needed to be in the industry and/or are very heavily regulated (e.g., electric utilities, airlines, or health care). In the oligopolistic market situation, the individual firms do have some control over prices and can create differentiation or vie for more of the market share by having price be part of their consumer acquisition strategy but not the sole differentiator.

MONOPOLY

Unlike the board game, a monopoly exists in the private enterprise system when there is absolutely no other competition. That means that there is only one provider that exists to provide a good or service, and usually it is the government that regulates who can enter the market, thereby creating extremely high barriers to entry. The lack of competition yields considerable power over prices in monopoly. An example of a pure monopoly is the issuance of a patent for a drug, in the case of a pharmaceutical company. Some pharmaceutical drugs have no current substitute, in which case the patent holder pharmaceutical company has a monopoly in the production/distribution of that drug. In this case, the government guarantees that no other company can produce the drug, and that provides a sufficient market entry barrier.

PLANNED ECONOMIES

In addition to the private enterprise system, planned economies are another market structure in the world economy. In a planned economy, government controls determine business ownership, profits, and resource allocation. Countries that existed with planned economies, however, have not been highly successful.

The most common theory of a planned economy is Communism, which purports that all property is shared equally by the people in a community under the direction of a strong central government. It is an economic system that involves government ownership of businesses. Rather than entrepreneurs, the government decides what products consumers will be offered and in what quantities. As the central planner, the government establishes trade policies that historically have been very restrictive in allowing foreign companies the opportunity to compete. Communism was proposed by Karl Marx and developed and implemented by V. I. Lenin. In Marxist theory, Communism denotes the final stage of human historical development in which the people rule both politically and economically.

The Communist philosophy is based on each individual contributing to the nation's overall economic success, and the country's resources are distributed according to each person's needs. The central government owns the means of production, and everyone works for state-owned enterprises. Further, the government determines what people can buy because it dictates what is produced.

Looking specifically at China and Russia, we can see what led to the failure of Communism. First of all, their constitutions had little or no meaning, so although the government created laws, they bore no power. Second, the government owned the means of production and made all of the economic decisions. Therefore, market forces were not allowed to work, and the laws of supply and demand were not followed. Third, the citizens of these countries had limited rights and all the citizens were subject to Communist party control. Individuals existed to serve the state and had virtually no freedom for themselves. All of these factors contributed to the downfall of communism, and as a result, China and Russia have more recently been "privatizing" and borrowing other capitalistic methods in an attempt to improve their economic situations and convert more to a market-based economy. They are desperately trying to get the market to find an equilibrium for their goods and services that we all too often take for granted.

SOCIALISM

Another economic system is socialism, which is characterized by government ownership and operation of major industries. For example, when telecommunications, petrol, or some other major industry is owned by the government, this is considered socialistic economy. Socialism is an economic system that contains some features of both capitalism and communism. Socialist governments allow people to own businesses and property and to select their own jobs. However, these governments are involved in providing a variety of public services, such as generous unemployment benefits, comprehensive health care for all citizens, and public transit. These public services are paid for by high tax rates on income. Entrepreneurs, not surprisingly, have less incentive to establish businesses if the tax rates are excessively high.

Socialism is based on the belief that major industries are too important to a society to be left in private hands; however, private ownership is allowed in industries considered to be less crucial to social welfare.

As socialism is retreating, there are new theories of regulation emerging. The new theories aren't aiming to regulate economic relations between individuals, as socialism did, but rather they seek to regulate social relations in general. For example, there is a desire to increase the social capital in communities. If *social capital* is defined as norms and networks that encourage cooperation and trust between individuals, then the existence of social capital can be beneficial. It reduces transaction costs, assists the diffusion of knowledge, and can enhance the sense of community well-being. The questions arising now, however, are whether the government can create social capital and, even more fundamental, whether the government *should* create social capital. Although the traditional form of socialism is no longer touted as a successful market structure, remnants of it can still be seen in today's economy.

The majority of market economies that we see today, however, are mixed market economies. These are economic systems that display characteristics of both planned and market economies. In the mixed market economy, government-owned firms frequently operate alongside private enterprises. Good examples of this can be found in Europe, where the respective governments have traditionally controlled certain key industries such as railroads, banking, and telecommunications. What is seen today, however, is a trend toward privatizing many of these state-owned industries. In 1986, the UK privatized the gas industry, in 1987 the steel industry, and in 1989 water was privatized. Today, Austria is following suit and is proceeding with the privatization of steel, oil, and chemicals.

FOUR STAGES OF THE BUSINESS CYCLE

The business cycle, also called the economic cycle, refers to the recurring series of events of expansion, boom, bust, and recession. The length of business cycles over time are rarely alike. The business cycle experiences periodic cyclical expansions and contractions in overall economic activity. For example, the United States has experienced eleven complete business cycles since the end of World War II. Business cycles are relevant because business decisions and consumer buying patterns differ at each stage of the business cycle, and it's important to know where you are in a business cycle when developing your organizational strategy.

Prosperity, or the "boom" part of the business cycle, occurs when unemployment is low, strong consumer confidence leads to record purchases, and as a result, businesses expand to take advantage of the opportunities created by the market. A good example of the market experiencing prosperity took place in Silicon Valley from 1998 to 2001. Suddenly the market identified technology as the next big business opportunity, so companies were adopting on-line technologies at a record pace; brick and mortar businesses were creating electronic marketplaces for the first time. As common sense tells us, no economy can sustain a boom forever, and as we saw in Silicon Valley, a recession, and sometimes a spot-depression, can follow the prosperity stage.

A *recession* is a cyclical economic contraction that lasts for at least six months. Economists agree that a recession results in a downturn lasting for at least two consecutive quarters. During a recession, consumers frequently postpone major purchases, such as homes and vehicles, and businesses slow production, postpone expansion plans, reduce inventories, and cut workers. As a result, unemployment rises and consumer demand decreases.

A *depression* is classified as a recession, or economic slowdown, that continues in a downward spiral over an extended period of time. It is also characterized by continued high unemployment and low consumer spending. Many economists suggest that sufficient government tools are available to prevent even a severe recession from turning into a depression. For example, federal, state, and local governments can make investments to improve the country's infrastructure as a means of bringing the market out of a depression. They can invest in transportation systems, public facilities such as schools and universities, or perhaps they can loan money to small businesses to help the economy grow. Governments can also influence the economy through regulations in fiscal and monetary policy, which will be discussed in more detail later in this chapter.

Eventually, these tools contribute to the next stage in the business cycle: recovery. The recovery period is when economic activity begins to pick up. Consumer confidence improves, which leads to increased spending on big items such as homes and vehicles. Unemployment also begins to fall, and people are working and contributing to the economy again.

THE STABILITY OF A NATION'S ECONOMY: PRODUCTIVITY, PRICE-LEVEL CHANGES, AND EMPLOYMENT LEVELS

By now we've seen how economies are the result of an interrelated mixture of numerous forces. The GDP, or gross domestic product, is the value of all goods and services produced within a nation's borders each year. It is a very popular economic indicator and provides a benchmark for the nation's overall economic activity.

Productivity is the relationship between the goods and services produced and the inputs needed to produce them. During expansionary periods, productivity tends to rise as fewer resources are needed to produce greater levels of output. During recessions, then, productivity might stagnate or decrease overall.

Price-level changes are related to the value of the economy's currency as well as inflation, a period of rising prices caused by a combination of excess demand and increases in the costs of the factors of production. In the United States, the rate of inflation is usually measured as the percentage change in the consumer price index, which includes the prices of a wide variety of consumer goods and services in categories such as food, clothing, medical services, housing, and transportation.

Demand-pull inflation occurs when there is an excess of demand relative to supply. In these conditions, a relative shortage of products or services gives producers the leverage to increase prices. Cost-push inflation occurs when there are rises in the costs of the factors of production. The costs of labor, commodities, manufacturing, and so on, rise and push prices up to cover the increased costs.

Hyperinflation is a period characterized by rapidly rising prices. Most people remember the images of people from Communist Russia standing in long lines to purchase bread because of hyperinflationary costs.

Inflation impacts the economy because more money is needed to sustain a given standard of living. If people receive a fixed income and suddenly the cost of bread increases dramatically, it is easy to see the negative impact caused by the rapidly increasing price of bread.

Inflation can be good news, though, to those who are experiencing a rising income or those with debts at fixed interest rates. Businesses, however, find it difficult to make long-range plans in high inflationary conditions, because budgeting and forecasting depend largely on confidently knowing the price of products and services needed to conduct business. Low inflation, on the other hand, makes it easier for businesses to make long-term plans—it becomes easier to predict prices and costs. Low inflation is also associated with low interest rates, encouraging major purchases by consumers and fueling business expansion.

Deflation is the price-level change referred to during a period of falling prices. While deflation sounds good, it can have disastrous consequences; the Great Depression was a general period of deflation, when prices fell, but so did employment, wages for those lucky enough to be employed, as well as most goods and services.

Relative price levels are measured by two common indicators. The Consumer Price Index (CPI) measures the monthly average change in the prices of a basket of goods and specific services and the Producer Price Index (PPI) looks at prices from the seller's perspective (finished goods, intermediate goods, and crude goods).

EMPLOYMENT LEVELS

Employment levels have a major impact on a nation's economy. In fact, the unemployment rate is one of the most relied-upon economic indicators that most people intuitively use to understand the state of the economy. The unemployment rate is usually expressed as the percentage of total workers who are actively seeking work but are currently unemployed.

Because the unemployment rate is so important, it's important to look more closely at different categories to describe variations of unemployment.

Frictional unemployment is when someone is temporarily not working. A good example is a recent graduate who is looking for work but has yet to find a job. *Seasonal unemployment* occurs when people are not working during some months, but they are not looking for a job during that period. People involved in the tourism industry or seasonal farmworkers are good examples of this. *Structural unemployment* results when people are not working because there is no demand for their particular skill set. An example might be auto workers in Detroit, where major manufacturers moved their assembly plants to other states or to other countries. There is a relatively low demand for people with an auto manufacturing skill set, so structural unemployment results for many in that field. People who fall into this category, however, may be training for a new job and developing new skills while they look for work. *Cyclical unemployment* results when there is an economic slowdown and people are looking for work but there aren't enough jobs. This was the case for many MBAs who graduated during the Great Recession of 2008.

The unemployment rate does not include the so-called discouraged workers, people who no longer have jobs and who are no longer looking for a job.

FACTORS AFFECTING GLOBAL ECONOMIES

In an ever-increasingly global economy, organizations are looking across borders and across continents to grow or sustain their economic future. In doing so, an organization's decision-makers look at an international expansion from a few perspectives.

POLITICAL RISK

Political risk represents the risk that another country's political actions may adversely affect a business. Carried to an extreme, a foreign government may take over a US firm's foreign subsidiary without compensating the US firm. A more common risk is the threat of higher tax rates or restrictions on the repatriation of profits to the US parent firm. In general, large-scale political events—such as military coups, social unrest, and currency crises—are referred to as macropolitical risks. Conversely, small-scale events—such as expropriation, discriminatory regulation, and terrorism—are referred to as micro-political risks.

CURRENCY RISK

Organizations looking to expand internationally face risk related to fluctuations in exchange rates. Currency risk is the risk of an investment's value changing because of change in the currency exchange rates, for example, a weak dollar is likely to increase both foreign sales and profits. These results are due to the lowering of the selling price of the exported goods, because fewer units of the foreign currency are now required to purchase US-made goods or services. A strong dollar is likely to decrease exports and profits. The appreciation of the US dollar against a foreign currency causes the purchase price of US goods abroad to increase; it now takes more units of the foreign currency to buy a given amount of US-made goods.

MONETARY AND FISCAL POLICY: MANAGING AN ECONOMY'S PERFORMANCE

Monetary policy is the regulation of the money supply and interest rates by a central bank, such as the US Federal Reserve (the Fed), in order to control inflation and stabilize currency. In the United States, the Fed is responsible for managing this process. If the economy is heating up, the Fed can withdraw money from the banking system, raise the reserve requirement, or raise the discount rate to make the economy cool down. This is referred to as a restrictive monetary policy and slows economic growth. If growth is slowing, the Fed can reverse the process—increase the money supply, lower the reserve requirement, and decrease the discount rate. This is referred to as an expansionary monetary policy, with lower interest rates.

Fiscal policy is the decision that the government makes to spend money or increase taxes for the specific purpose of stabilizing the economy. Government increases in spending or lowering of taxes tend to stimulate economic growth, while decreasing government spending or increasing taxes tend to slow economic growth.

THE US ECONOMY IN AN INTERNATIONAL CONTEXT AND THE DEVELOPMENT OF A GLOBAL MIND-SET

As our economies and policies become increasingly interrelated across borders and oceans, we face a more complex economic picture. The globalized economy has brought many challenges and opportunities to organizations and communities.

Successful new businesses are now being "conceived globally," seeking cross borders business and development from the outset. Today's organizations, throughout their ranks, must have a global mind-set that recognizes, utilizes, and respects cultural, societal, and aspirational differences across nations, beliefs, and social systems.

To succeed in the long run and improve financial stability, organizations will seek a global mind-set by:

- Competing in another environment, often far away from its organizational roots

- Expanding and innovating globally, not by just exporting existing products or services but by adapting to global markets and their cultural norms
- Diversifying leadership: as organizations develop and widen worldwide markets, its leadership must also reflect its global footprint
- Global citizenry: business will need to interact, respect, and cooperate with governments and stakeholders with sensitivity to regulatory, social, and trade issues

The opportunities that go along with this more global picture are great, but so too are the challenges. Cell phones, computers, disease-resistant crops, satellites, biotechnology, and fiber-optic networks are among the twentieth-century technologies that will shape political, social, and economic realities well into the twenty-first century—realities that include the continuing globalization of business, culture, and health care. So what are the challenges?

INTERNATIONAL TERRORISM

It used to be that international terrorism happened to Americans only when we were not on our home turf. September 11, however, showed us that we are no longer safe within our own borders. Terrorist attacks are becoming more lethal too. Most terrorist organizations active in the 1970s and 1980s had clear political objectives. They tried to calibrate their attacks to produce just enough bloodshed to get attention for their cause, but not so much as to alienate public support. Today, as we have seen, the objectives are increasingly religious, economic, or personal (against an ethnic group) in nature.

Economics, technology, and the whims of both criminals and zealots will produce ongoing and, at times, spectacular events. Sadly, terrorism in the Third World and developing countries has continued and spawned new forms, modalities, and targets. Cyber terrorism is an ever-increasing concern, with damage and threats previously only associated with physical, brute force terrorism.

SHIFT TO A GLOBAL INFORMATION ECONOMY

The information economy is affecting supply chains, digital technologies, information and communication technologies, and technology-enabled marketing, pushing businesses to go wireless, changing organizational structures, and increasing the value of intellectual property.

Some think the movement to an information economy is being oversold as the key to economic opportunity. Information technology can help people learn how to absorb knowledge generated elsewhere and combine it with local needs and local knowledge and may help raise economic returns to investments, but these are still more familiar development challenges (e.g., structural unemployment, social inequality, and an undereducated workforce).

AGING OF THE WORLD'S POPULATION AND SLOWER POPULATION GROWTH

The world's population is getting older and older as a result of dropping fertility rates and urbanization. Europe provides an excellent example of how the aging population is changing policy and business. Fertility rates have plummeted, especially in southern Europe, to the point that every ten Italian women are expected to have just twelve children in their lifetime, and every ten Spanish women just eleven. As a group, the countries of the EU are going to see their populations shrink unless they allow significant levels of immigration.

The situation in Europe is not unique to Europe. In fact, well over half of the world's elderly (age sixty-five and older) now live in developing nations, and this is projected to grow to 71 percent by 2030. Many developing countries have had a significant downturn in their rate of natural population increase, and as this process gets faster and faster, age structures will change.

CONSUMERS

It is important to consider that businesses ultimately fail or succeed because of consumer preferences and their ability to satisfy such preferences. Whether a business provides a product or service to the end user or to an intermediary, whether or not a product or service is chosen will depend upon consumer preferences. Part of what goes into the consumers' choice is the perception of quality.

US consumers have the perception that certain foreign-made goods are of higher quality than US-made goods. In the past, this has been true, for example, of cars and electronic goods made in Japan. French wine and Swiss watches are other examples of goods that some US consumers believe are better than similar domestic products.

SUMMARY

Creating a long-term global strategy is complicated and complex; no country is an economic island and the economy truly is global. A growing number of businesses have become true multinational firms, with operating facilities around the world. They have figured out how to mitigate their risks both politically and economically, but they have also found how events in one nation can reverberate around the world.

As US businesses contemplate and engage in global expansion, there are endless opportunities but also potential risks. The US market is also attractive to foreign firms. For an organization to be successful in today's global economy, its owners and stakeholders must look across borders and understand the global community.

Section III

MARKETS AND STRATEGY

Chapter 9

MARKETING, STRATEGY, AND COMPETITIVE ANALYSIS

W e've all heard someone say, "Marketing is fluff and hype." However, the wisest, most savvy, and ultimately successful businesspeople understand that marketing is far from that. Marketing is everything you do on a daily basis to sell a product or provide a service to a customer. Marketing considers every way in which a customer perceives a business and everything that generates enough interest from a customer and encourages customers to actually pay for the product or service. As Peter Vessenes suggests, "Cash may be king, but marketing is everything."

What does it really mean to market a service or product? Often, people immediately equate marketing with advertising and see only the amount of money that advertising will cost. However, by definition, marketing is actually the process by which we offer goods or services up for sale. Forward-thinking marketing strategists suggest that marketing is not a cost or expense but rather an investment, because much of the benefit of marketing is longer term and may take years to fully come to fruition.

Marketing has also been referred to as a social and managerial process by which individuals and groups obtain what they need and want through creating, offering, and exchanging products of value with others. Additionally, it is all too often equated only with the more focused function of "selling." But marketing encompasses a wider range of activities that must be a fully integrated process and, indeed, will form a foundation and catalyst for making sales. Further, the key to successful sales is a consistent, proactive marketing strategy.

MARKETING'S KEY OBJECTIVE: CREATING VALUE FOR THE CUSTOMER

What then is the key to a consistent proactive marketing strategy? First and foremost, it is a philosophy that dedicates resources of the firm to ensuring that the wants, needs, and demands of the customer are the firm's focus. This customer-focused mentality is the foundation of the strategy that makes up the entire marketing process.

Second, it is a plan, supported by the firm's philosophy. Once the philosophy is in place, a plan can give direction, guidance, and a structure for proactive strategies that will increase sales and improve business relationships. Often firms find themselves dedicating resources to marketing activities—from tradeshows to fliers—and spending money on marketing that is not targeted to the right audience at the right time. This is reactive marketing with a shotgun, rather than a rifle.

Conversely, a proactive, focused marketing plan can provide guidance for targeting the right audience at the right place and at the right time, which in turn maximizes the return on investment and increasing revenues.

Third, marketing is a process of creating value for the customer. It is a set of activities to educate, communicate with, and motivate the targeted consumer about the firm's services or the company's products and services.

Traditionally, this set of activities, the marketing mix, is represented by four parts, the well-known Four Ps of Marketing: Price, Product, Placement, and Promotion. But to create a marketing strategy and plan that touches on all areas necessary to position a product in the market to maximize sales revenues, multiple areas must be tackled. An effective marketing strategy/plan is an ongoing value-creating process composed of several elements:

MARKET SEGMENTATION

One of the first steps in developing an overall marketing strategy is to perform a market segmentation analysis as a way to manage the strategy development process and insure its effectiveness and success. The concept behind market segmentation is intuitive and relatively simple. Market segmentation is simply taking a look at the overall market for your product and service and thinking of it in terms of smaller, more manageable pieces.

Think of market segmentation as what Bert and Ernie from Sesame Street sing about when they suggest "…one of these things is not like the other…one of these things doesn't belong…" In a sense, that's what we are doing when we segment a market—we are looking at the whole and trying to determine how we can group the mass market into smaller groups that, while they are different from each other, are more alike within the groups.

Once we have identified these subgroupings, we can target which of these "market segments" are likely to be the most productive and the best fit with our company's strengths and competitive advantages.

A well-used example of market segmentation is the way the players in the hospitality industry look at the market for hotel/motel rooms. Rather than take a "one size fits all" approach to this market, a company like Marriott looks at the overall market and segments it into several smaller, but more focused, market segments. For the "travel and leisure" segment of the overall hotel/motel market, Marriott's Fairfield Inn is located near major tourist attractions, is budget-priced, and appeals to families. For the middle-level manager who travels a lot and wants some comforts of home while on the road, the Courtyard by Marriott is located near businesses and has a residential, feels-like-home atmosphere. For CEOs and top-level executives, Marriott's Ritz-Carlton has all the upscale amenities and top-level customer service that presidents and CEOs of business and industry are used to and expect when they travel. Note that in these examples, Marriott has broken this overall, mass market into more manageable, more focused segments, and importantly, note how its marketing strategy for each segment is tailored to that segment.

By applying the principles of market segmentation, a marketer can make better use of his or her marketing budget and more efficiently manage the company's overall marketing strategy.

MARKETING STRATEGY

To build a strong and durable house, it is necessary to create blueprints. Likewise, to build a strong and profitable business, it is necessary to develop a strategy. Essentially, a marketing strategy is a plan that allows an organization to direct activities that are consistent with the goals of the organization and spend money wisely in order to create the greatest amount of return on investment.

MARKET RESEARCH AND COMPETITIVE INTELLIGENCE

To thoroughly understand what is happening in the industry in which an organization operates, it's invaluable to know what the trends in the industry are as well as what the firm's competitors are doing to make money, to improve their business, and to improve their own market share.

Market research is necessary to make better firm-wide decisions. With marketing being a philosophy where the resources and activities of the firm or company are focused on satisfying the wants and needs of the customer, marketing research is the way an organization with a marketing philosophy determines what those wants and needs may be and, further, how to communicate the associated benefits most effectively and efficiently.

Additionally, market research is used to monitor and modify, if needed, the elements of the marketing strategy. Market research includes defining the problem and research objectives, developing a research plan, presenting the plan, implementing the plan (collecting and analyzing data), and interpreting and reporting the findings. This is the area of marketing where we begin to see science, as well as art.

PRICING

To sell a product for a particular price, value must be created. Value is the consumer's estimate of the product's overall capacity to satisfy his or her needs. When the value placed on a product or service is high, then satisfaction is achieved. Consumers are savvy and will choose based on the level of satisfaction that corresponds with the price. If one bottle of Coke is priced at five dollars, while a whole liter of Pepsi is priced at one dollar, it is likely that the sales of Coke will decrease. If these are the only two options at the supermarket, the likelihood of Pepsi sales increasing is high.

Pricing is what a potential customer is willing to trade in return for a product, the value he or she places on a product or service. Generally, a price/quality relationship exists—the higher the price, the higher the quality. Especially in the case of personal services, consumers will expect a higher level of service if the fee associated with that service is higher relative to other providers of similar services.

Marketers may elect to "skim" the market with a relatively high price at first and then, as demand wanes at this relatively high price, gradually lower the price. New, innovative products often use this pricing strategy because their newness and uniqueness may enable a higher price at first. As copycats and competitors enter the market, prices will fall to meet the market price.

Some marketers may use a "penetration" strategy, where the product or service is offered at a very low price as a strategy to quickly grab market share and be considered the low price provider. Walmart is an example of a company using a penetration pricing strategy.

Pricing is a powerful tool in developing a marketing strategy with a strong connection to the financial condition of the organization. Pricing too low may result in economic consequences if costs are not covered, and pricing too high may stunt demand and sales of the product or service, also resulting in economic consequences.

PLACEMENT

A customer will not likely purchase a service or product unless it can be relatively easily accessed. Placement can be anything from a magazine or candy bar sitting next to the check-out counter at the supermarket—a spontaneous purchase—to gas stations situated on the right-hand corner of the exit from a highway or to the location of an orthodontist's office in the same building as a pediatrician's office.

Placement helps make the purchasing process for a customer easier and more convenient. Often the term *distribution* is used interchangeably for the placement component of a marketing strategy and includes the decisions a company or firm must make to ensure the connection with the customer or client. Placement is how the marketer connects the products or services with the customer—the easier, more convenient, and more accessible the product or service may be, the more likely the customer will purchase the product or service.

THE VALUE CHAIN

All of the above-mentioned parts of the marketing plan cannot be carried out to the full level of effectiveness without all areas, a value chain, working together. Generally, the value chain includes the following activities:

- Inbound logistics: bringing raw materials into the business
- Operations: management of processes to create the product or service for the customer
- Outbound logistics: the means for getting the product or service to the customer (for example, distribution systems and shippers to get products into retail stores)
- Marketing and sales: creating value
- Service: aligning customer expectations and the performance of the product or service
- Firm infrastructure: the organization of the firm to maximize service to the customer
- Human resources management: creating a structure for the people in the firm, which includes recruitment, training, retention, and compensation of employees
- Technology: using technology to maximize service, thereby enhancing customer value

BRANDING, ADVERTISING, PROMOTION, AND SOCIAL MEDIA

Every day we are bombarded with different advertising messages, whether it is on the radio while we're driving to work, on television during our favorite programs, on our computer or smartphone screens, or in magazines and newspapers. We're handed fliers while walking down the streets and given tastes of products while walking the aisles of the grocery store. Advertising has entered every area of our lives, and many of us choose to ignore it on many occasions. This brings up the question, can advertising and promotional efforts still be effective if we are so saturated with information?

The answer is yes, advertising and promotions can be effective if used properly for targeting the right consumer. One of the main rules in advertising has always been to keep your message simple and consistent and repeat it often. It has been shown that people remember advertising if they see it with great frequency, which explains why the same advertisement might be shown two or even three times during two hours of television. The message will reside in the mind of viewers that way.

BRANDING

On the shelves of every grocery store are brand-name products from Oreo cookies to Tide detergent. Strong brands are a great asset to a company and can generate streams of incremental revenue due to the fact that people are willing to pay a premium for brand-name products, and, over time, that reduces marketing costs because a brand's loyal customers present lower or no purchase barriers.

A brand is a name, symbol, term, sign, design, or combination of each of these things, the purpose of which is to identify goods and services of one seller or of a group of sellers and differentiate them from competitors. A brand is also the sum of all characteristics that make a product offering unique. A company can copy a product, but they cannot replicate the brand. In a sense, the brand is the "personality" of the product, what the product "means" to the customer and the set of emotions evoked when the brand is encountered or used by the customer.

BRAND IDENTITY

A brand's identity is the company's vision of the brand and the brand's promise to consumers. It is also the outward visible identity of the corporate brand or family of brands. McDonald's, for example, has the golden arches as part of its brand identity, but it also represents convenience and products with a level of consistent quality. When you order a McDonald's cheeseburger, it should taste the same whether you are ordering it in Los Angeles, Hartford, Shanghai, or Moscow, and it should be prepared quickly, because it is "fast food." On the other hand, because of McDonald's long-enduring branding strategy, its customers know it's not the place to go for outstanding veal scaloppini.

BRAND IMAGE

The brand image is the consumer's perception of the brand. Companies will try to bridge the gap between brand identity and brand image. Consistency is the key element when promoting a brand or product, and a clear and consistent promotional campaign will help ensure that the brand's image and the brand identity are very similar.

BRAND LOYALTY

People who only buy a particular brand of product or service are considered by marketers to be "brand loyal." There are various levels of brand loyalty, from extremely loyal to brand terrorist and everything in between. Think about the products consumers buy; are they willing to purchase any brand of detergent or coffee creamer? Some people will only use Clorox bleach or Coffeemate coffee creamer, others will be satisfied using private label bleach or a generic creamer and may not notice a difference beyond price. Others may be loyal some of the time; however, if there is a sale or promotion, their buying habits may change, and they may switch to another competitive product. For example a consumer may buy Coke regularly, but would he or she buy Pepsi instead if there were a sale? If so, those consumers are not brand loyal to either Coke or Pepsi, and they be capable of switching.

When a consumer has a bad experience with a brand-name product or service, they may tell others about their dissatisfaction; these people are deemed "brand terrorists" and may act as an adverse multiplier of reputation. A rule of thumb is that a positive experience will have a one- or two-time positive effect, but customers with a negative experience will tell eight to ten people. If a consumer has a terrible meal at a local restaurant, chances are not only will he or she not eat at the restaurant again, but also he or she will tell friends or family about that negative experience. The same can be true with your experience with any kind of product. People who have a bad experience with a brand, product, or service are much more likely to express their dissatisfaction with their experience than those who have good experiences.

While there is no way of ensuring that every person is completely satisfied, companies take measures to try to please their customers through high levels of customer service. They can also take steps to win over customers from other products or services in order to compensate for lost customers with new customers.

INTEGRATED MARKETING COMMUNICATIONS

A theme that emerged from the exploration of branding was the importance of consistency. Organizations ensure the consistency of their brand value and message by coordinating all of their promotional activities so they reinforce each other and deliver a consistent image and message. This coordination of activities into a system or strategic plan is referred to as Integrated Marketing Communications (IMC).

IMC creates a unified message and enhances the effectiveness of reaching the target consumer. Firms will create one message that will be used consistently throughout a marketing campaign. It is important that the promotional strategy also be in alignment with the organizational goals.

There are four major aspects of an IMC plan: research, creative aspects, planning, and implementation.

- *Research and analysis* are used to find the best way to design the product or service, the most effective message and media to use, and the best means to distribute the product or service at the optimal price.

- The *creative aspect* is the actual advertising, copywriting, and designing of promotional materials.
- *Planning* an integrated marketing communications plan also means finding your target market; determining what is unique about the product offering or service you are providing; constructing a positioning strategy for your product or service (building a mental niche in relation to competitor products or services); deciding what the best message would be for your product; choosing the optimal marketing mix in relation to your allowed marketing budget.
- *Implementation* is the act of putting the plan together, creating a strategy, and seeing it through.

Marketers of consumer products, especially in crowded markets deploy IMC because buying decisions are better influenced when there are multiple touch points and messaging contact points.

Most IMC marketers begin with extensive research about their target customers: media choices, attitudinal profiles, lifestyle choices, etc. Informed by this intelligence, they will create promotional messaging and images for use in traditional print, digital, or social media. They may also deploy other ways to maintain contact with customers such as sponsoring events that attract viewers and participants consistent with the target customer. Whether it's NASCAR as way to reach blue-collar, working family demographics or a PGA golf tournament as a way to reach high income, professionals, marketers are integrating these promotional efforts into their overall marketing strategy to build a consistent and synergistic approach in connecting with their customer base.

Ideally, an effective IMC campaign will differentiate the product or service from a competitor's; generate a flow of leads (which are the predecessor to sales); be consistent with and support the overall branding strategy; communicate the company's experience and knowledge; and help to retain existing customers.

THE PROMOTIONAL MIX

The promotional mix is the use of different advertising and communication methods in a coordinated way to run an effective marketing campaign. These coordinated campaigns are part of an effective integrated marketing communications plan. The four main methods of promotion within the mix are advertising, sales promotion, personal selling, and public relations.

The most important factor in determining the optimal mix is identifying the target market. This can be determined through extensive market research. Once an organization finds its target market, it can then research its use of various media outlets in order to come up with the best combination of marketing materials to reach the defined target. For example, if the target market is stay-at-home moms, an organization might find that television advertisements during certain daytime television shows is most effective for reaching them. If the target market is young professionals, the marketer might find that using billboards in a downtown commercial district and morning drive-time radio advertisements is effective for getting their message across.

The size of the promotional budget will greatly influence the chosen mix as well. Television advertising can be very costly and, therefore, may not be a feasible option for a company with a smaller marketing budget, at least not during prime viewing hours on major networks. Often the amount of money a firm spends on promotional activities will be affected by the product life cycle, general economic conditions, and the competition.

The promotional mix may involve a company coordinating its loyalty program with advertising campaigns and a promotional deal. For example, an airline may deploy an e-mail blast to its frequent flyers advertising five thousand free bonus miles for booking a ticket in the next month. In this instance, the airline is coordinating a digital approach via its loyalty program membership for a promotional campaign.

ADVERTISING

Advertising is paid communication brought to audiences through different forms of media such as television, radio, newspapers, webpages and Internet, magazines, and billboards. Companies use advertising to inform, persuade, or remind their target markets of their products or services.

Comparative advertising is a use of advertising to differentiate a company's products in the marketplace from other similar products. For example, McDonald's and Burger King used to run comparative advertising, comparing their cooking methods for hamburgers. The "Pepsi Challenge" campaign was another form of comparative advertising in which consumers were asked to take blind taste tests to see if they could tell the difference between the products.

Reminder advertising is used once a product has matured in the marketplace and has already achieved a high level of brand identification. Coca-Cola uses reminder ads to show how refreshing their beverage can be on a hot day, and Budweiser wants to remind the consumer to "Make it a Bud night." Some ads use nostalgia to remind viewers about their childhood enjoyment of a product such as Oreo Cookies, and although their taste buds may have matured, they can still enjoy them.

Institutional advertising promotes the company, organization, government agency, or a concept or philosophy, but not a specific product. For example, ads for BASF, one of the world's largest manufacturers of chemicals and chemical related products, states, "We don't make a lot of the products you buy. We make a lot of the products you buy better." Another example is the army recruitment commercials that tell potential recruits, "Be all you can be."

Industry advertising promotes a whole industry rather than just one company or product. The most popular example of this is the "Got milk?" ad campaigns that were sponsored by the California Milk Processing Board.

Another example is the "Hanker for a hunk of cheese" campaign that was sponsored by the Wisconsin Dairy Board.

ADVERTISING MEDIUMS

There are advantages and disadvantages to each media type, and when selecting the advertising mediums to use, organizations must understand who their target audience is and the most effective method for reaching them. It is quite a challenge to allocate marketing budgets among the myriad of media choices. On one hand, there's value in a very diversified assortment of media, but that may mean a little bit of spending across a lot of media with a possible outcome being a relatively weak presence in each of the chosen media types. If an organization "puts all its eggs in one or two baskets" and places its entire marketing budget in one or two media forms, they may be getting a big impact from the one or two media choices, but they're missing targeted customers who may be otherwise reachable via other unutilized media choices.

TELEVISION

Television advertising is historically the leading medium for reaching US audiences. Although a very expensive form of advertising, television ads reach the largest percentage of the US population at once and can be very appealing due to their visual nature as well as their sound.

TV ads can be classified into national, local, and cable advertisements. The type of network chosen will depend on which audience the marketer is trying to reach. If the advertisement is for a local restaurant, the company may choose to advertise only on local stations or in local ad space on cable channels or national networks. Companies targeting Hispanics may choose to advertise on a Spanish-language cable station such as Telemundo or advertise during a television show whose viewing audience is predominantly Hispanic.

The time an advertisement is shown is also an important decision that companies must make in order to reach the target audience. Budgetary constraints will also be a factor in choosing time slots for advertisements. Super Bowl ads are extremely expensive but can be cost effective for reaching an audience of sports fans. On the other hand, a television ad exists only during the ten, thirty, or sixty seconds it appears, so to keep the message alive in the mind of the target customer, most television ad campaigns require multiple airings, resulting in very high cost, not only for the air time but also for high-quality production to increase the likelihood of recall and "share of mind," or the ability for a product or service to gain favorable retention in a potential customer's mind when a buying decision occurs after the television ad is viewed.

PRINT ADS

Advertising in newspapers and magazines is another way of reaching customers with a company's message. Print ads are effective because of their visual quality and can be run in many different types of publications. Marketers selling products or services to consumers may choose national publications such as *Time* magazine or local newspapers such as the *Chicago Tribune*. Businesses trying to sell products or services to other businesses will often advertise in trade publications of the industries they are trying to reach. Companies may also target specialized publications; for example, a new computer product may be advertised in *PC World* or another specialty technology publication. Print ads have a longer "life" than electronic media ads and are good for "telling a story" about the value of a product or service.

RADIO

Although lacking the visual appeal, radio can be an effective medium for reaching target consumers. The average radio listener tunes in for three hours a day, and often on a regular basis. When using radio advertisements in a promotion mix, it is necessary to make sure that the company and product or service is clearly identified. As with television, it is also necessary to find the right station for advertising to the target consumer. If an organization's service is a bar for college-aged students, they may choose to advertise in the evenings on a college station or an alternative rock station; if the target audience is senior citizens, then it may be advantageous to advertise on news stations or a talk show.

DIRECT MAIL

Mailing advertisements or promotions directly to people's homes is another commonly used method of reaching consumers. Direct mail campaigns can be expensive, due to printing and postage costs, but these campaigns can be effective if the mailings reach the right consumers, and, importantly, tracking effectiveness of a direct mail campaign is relatively easy if the campaign includes coupons or promotional codes. Often companies will purchase lists of consumers or collect data themselves to build a mailing list. The people on these lists will then be sent targeted mailings.

TELEMARKETING

The utilization of telemarketing has been affected in the United States by the national "Do Not Call" registry, however this method is still being deployed, especially for political marketing. The downside of telemarketing is that most people do not like the invasiveness of being called at home, though mass marketers find the risk of offending nonreceptive households offset by the effective results and benefits of telemarketing.

OUTDOOR AND "OUT OF HOME"

The majority of outdoor advertising dollars is spent on billboards. Billboards are a popular way of reaching commuters and consumers in a single geographic location. Digital billboards are providing this "old school" advertising method with an opportunistic update. With digital billboards, advertisers can update their billboard message and design quickly and make the billboard as up to date as the news feed on their computer or smartphone. For the digital billboard supplier, digital provides the opportunity to serve multiple customers on the same billboard, with the billboard ad "rotating" several times per minute. Other forms of outdoor advertising (known as "out of home") include sports stadium ads, bus shelter posters, or signage on buses and taxis.

ADVERTISING TRENDS

Many advertisers use celebrities and are willing to allocate a large portion of their advertising budget to hire a celebrity to represent their brand. From William Shatner advertising cheap travel for Priceline.com to Tina Fey using an American Express card, celebrities are part of an advertising message and campaign. Of course, using a celebrity spokesperson can be a risk, for example, using O. J. Simpson as the Hertz Rental Car spokesperson.

When choosing a celebrity to endorse products, it is important to find an appropriate match with the product or service. The relationship should be believable. It is also important that the celebrities endorsing the product be credible; they should either have expertise in the field or be trustworthy characters.

SPONSORSHIPS

Another well-used form of promotion and advertising is sponsorships. Sponsorships are a form of advertising that allows the company to buy into a sporting event or activity. The amount of investment in a sponsorship can range from an athletic company supporting a college sports team by providing them with brand-name uniforms in order to promote the brand to a company sponsoring a college football bowl game. As in the case of celebrity endorsements, it is important for a good fit between the company's products or services and the nature of the event or activity being sponsored. Often an event sponsorship provides a bundle of benefits to the sponsor, such as admission tickets for clients, distribution of handouts or samples during the event, and visibility on scoreboards or banners seen by attendees and also by the television audience.

INFOMERCIALS

An infomercial is an extended television advertisement that usually runs at off-peak hours or on lower budget television or cable networks. They are usually at least a half hour long. Some of the most popular items that are sold through infomercials are fitness videos, skin care products, and kitchenware. Often they will feature celebrity endorsements and offer products that cannot be purchased in stores.

SALES PROMOTION

Sales promotion consists of many activities used to sell products. They are activities that give customers a short-term incentive to make a purchase. Sales promotions are also activities that change the price and value relationship of a product as perceived by the target audience with the possible effect of generating immediate sales. It is possible that sales promotion can also alter the long-term value of the brand by making what might be a "premium" product more affordable.

Sales promotions are generally time-bound programs that require participation on the part of the customer, either through immediate purchase or some other action. The fundamental goals of sales promotion are tactical, strategic, and ultimate. The tactical goals may be to combat a competitor's increase in market share, to combat other competitors' promotional efforts, or to move brands that are either declining, overstocked, damaged, or not selling fast enough. The strategic goals are to motivate consumers to switch from a rival brand, to increase product consumption, to reinforce the marketing communications efforts for the brand, and to motivate brand loyalty. The ultimate goal of a sales promotion is to increase sales, profits, and market share.

CONSUMER PROMOTIONS

Consumer promotions are geared toward getting consumers to try their products. Some examples of consumer promotion activities include rebates, coupons, sampling, point-of-purchase displays, sweepstakes, and "special packs."

Whether they're cut out from newspapers and magazines, received in the mail, or downloaded from a website, coupons are a very popular form of sales promotion. They are very effective, especially in economic downturns, for luring people into restaurants or causing them to make repeat purchases of products.

E-coupons are extremely effective for luring in customers and are redeemed by a high percent of the people who click on them. The most popular use of e-coupons is for sales of groceries, books, and health and music products.

The disadvantage of coupons is that they do not encourage brand loyalty; most consumers who use coupons regularly are willing to switch brands if there is a better discount available.

Rebates are refunds that are offered by the manufacturers. Often manufacturers will use mail-in or e-mail rebates as incentives for purchasing. The consumer must purchase the product at full price and then fill out paperwork and submit the receipt in order to receive the money. Rebate programs allow marketers to promote a product at a reduced, post-rebate price, offering a substantial savings to its customers, but also requiring that a set of conditions be met to qualify.

SAMPLING

Companies will often send or hand out samples of products in order to attract customers who may not have purchased their product otherwise. Beverage companies may target college students and hand out soft drinks on campuses, or a food company may set up a stand in a grocery store so that consumers can sample their new chips. The intention of these promotions is to introduce a new product or service to a consumer in order to generate brand loyalty. Sampling can be a costly method of attracting customers, and it often results in wasted distribution; however, it can be a very effective method for getting consumers to switch brands.

SWEEPSTAKES AND CONTESTS

Sweepstakes and contests are another type of sales promotion. Data will be collected from consumers, and they will be entered to win a prize. Companies can use the information they collect from entrants in order to develop a list for future promotional campaigns. Organizations must be sure to print all the guidelines for their sweepstakes or contest in order to avoid legal entanglements.

Some of the guidelines companies should follow in order to put on a successful sweepstakes include the following: clarify who is eligible; indicate states where the promotion is not valid; declare the termination date of the promotion; and clarify random drawing procedures. Companies should also detail the prizes; disclose the odds of winning; declare a deadline for entry; and reserve the right to use winners' names and photographs for publicity.

POINT OF PURCHASE DISPLAYS

Point of purchase (POP) promotional materials are displays that are set up in stores in order to prominently display products. At a grocery store, a POP is usually placed in the front of the store or at the end of an aisle, or it may be placed in the aisle or on the shelf. POP displays are very successful due to the fact that many people make last-minute purchasing decisions.

BUNDLING

Sometimes companies bundle products together in order to promote a new product or to encourage consumers to try a complimentary product, such as a free small conditioner bundled with a shampoo purchase, or a free disposable razor with a shaving cream purchase. A company may also offer a bonus pack or a special pack with 20 percent more in order to encourage a customer to purchase a product.

GIVEAWAYS

Another method used by companies is that of special promotional items (otherwise known as swag—Stuff We All Get) to be given away. These may be hats or T-shirts advertising the company or brand, such as when credit card companies offer T-shirts if you sign up for a new credit card. A beer company may be giving away pint glasses to customers who purchase their brand of beer on certain nights. Alcoholic beverage companies use representatives to go to concerts, bars, and clubs and promote their products by giving away promotional items.

TRADE PROMOTIONS

Trade promotions are geared toward marketing intermediaries in business-to-business relationships and are not as common in direct to consumer marketing. A snack food manufacturer, for example, may offer a discounted price to retailers if they buy a large quantity of a product. These types of promotions are most successful when they offer financial incentives and serve to effectively reduce the cost of the product.

Another form of trade promotion occurs when a brand is paying for shelf space in a retail store, inasmuch as placement is an important factor in consumer buying. Products at eye level on a retailer shelf have a higher rate of sales than similar products located near the floor. Brands are willing to pay a "slotting fee" in order to have their products prominently displayed on the desired shelf or in a preferred position within a retail store, such as on the end cap (the shelf space at the end of each row of shelves), because end caps have greater and more frequent views as consumers make their way through the store.

PERSONAL SELLING

Personal selling uses a personal sales presentation to influence customers to buy a product. Personal selling tactics are most often used when there are a few geographically concentrated customers, the product is highly technical in nature, the product is very expensive, or the product moves through direct distribution channels. It is a tactic often used by businesses looking to sell to other businesses, as opposed to businesses selling to consumers.

The sales process involves a personal seller identifying the target customer by determining who is likely to buy his or her product. Once the target customers have been identified, the salesperson will contact them. Upon meeting with potential customers, the salesperson will make a sales presentation, explaining how the customer needs the product or service that is being sold. The salesperson should be prepared to answer the customer's questions. After the presentation, the goal of the salesperson is to "close the sale" while the presentation is still fresh in the mind of the customer. Following up with the purchaser after the sale is a critical, but often overlooked, part of the sales process and is especially effective for developing long-term relationships.

RELATIONSHIP STRATEGIES

Developing an effective relationship strategy can be the key to forming long-term relationships with customers and in turn creating loyalty. Good customer service and treating customers fairly become the critical first steps for ensuring a healthy relationship. Fair treatment includes responding to customer complaints and finding workable solutions to resolving mistakes that have been made. Although the customer may not always be right, the customer should always be treated graciously. Serving customers well by providing them with truthful information and creating personable contact with them is critical.

A company's internal structure is also very important to its ability to build relationships with customers. The company should be running a cost-effective business, possess interpersonal skills, and have the technical know-how of its product offerings.

For many professional service providers, their staff may have more interaction with the client than the professional service provider, making it critical that the staff have the same level of concern for customer service and satisfaction as the provider.

For instance, for a doctor's appointment, the patient (customer) spends a lot of time on the phone to make the appointment, then with the receptionist, then likely with a nurse who's doing basic vital information measurements, and then, finally, with the doctor. And though the doctor may be well trained and provides good medical attention, the patient's overall satisfaction with his or her visit to the doctor's office may be negatively affected if the three or four other members of the doctor's office team do not treat the patient with the same care and concern as the doctor actually providing the medical attention that is the core reason for the office visit.

Additionally, it's very important that companies recognize who their most valuable customers are. Those are the customers who benefit the company the most through their purchases. Companies will want to focus their long-term relationship-building efforts on these types of customers, because it will be more profitable. In a competitive environment complicated by high marketing costs, most marketers are moving toward a relationship-building strategy of "greater share of customers" instead of "greater market share."

Many companies will use forms of customer relationship management in order to keep track of their customers' purchases, determine who their most profitable customers are, and target special promotions and product or service offers to their customers using the information they collect. Many banks are starting to offer these services, and you may notice that when you call to get account information the customer service representative will offer you other products. Phone companies have also taken up this practice. It can be a very successful way of introducing new products and services to existing customers, upselling customers, or influencing them to purchase more products.

PUBLIC RELATIONS AND PUBLICITY

An organization's public relations and publicity activities serve to foster its relationships with its various audiences and to communicate with them. Public relations efforts are undertaken in order to form a favorable view in the public eye.

Favorable publicity can enhance an organization's image and increase demand for its products. A positive article or review about a product or service adds credibility, believability, and legitimacy in a much more effective manner than "paid for" advertising. Negative publicity, on the other hand, can tarnish an organization's reputation. Most public relations strategies include: press releases, special events, and press conferences.

Press releases are articles or brief news releases that are submitted to publications by the firm. They often will provide information about company happenings: new hires, new products or services, or changes in management. They can be an effective way of gaining attention and creating or maintaining awareness.

Many organizations sponsor special events, such as a product launch. A fashion company may sponsor a fashion show to display its new line of clothing. A musician may hold a record release party for his or her new album. The firm will often invite top clientele, industry insiders, and media to these events.

A news conference is an in-person announcement of recent organizational events to the media. It is an effective method of informing the public of recent happenings without causing rumors to be spread, because the information will come straight from the source.

THE CRITICAL ROLE OF WEB-BASED MARKETING AND SOCIAL MEDIA

In order to market effectively via the Internet, an organization needs a web address that is relevant to its business and will form the foundation for its website.

Pick a domain name that describes the organization or includes the name of the organization. The explosive growth of the web has made it challenging to register a domain name exactly matched up to an organization's name. The key here is to pick a domain name that makes sense to website visitors and people looking for your organization's products or services. It is essential to pick a name that is easy to remember and is relatively short. If people cannot remember the domain name, it will be difficult for them to find you or return to your website.

SETTING E-MAIL SYSTEM

Since it serves as a communicating link between the organization and its website visitors, setting up e-mail addresses is as important as picking the right domain name. Don't forget to add a signature to e-mails. This signature should include contact information, such as phone and fax number; Facebook, LinkedIn, and Twitter profiles; and a web address with a direct link to the organization's home page.

THE CRITICAL MARKETING MISSION OF A WEBSITE

A well-designed and professional-looking website not only creates a visual appeal but also encourages web visitors to stay longer and prompts them to suggest the company to their friends.

THE VISUAL APPEAL: USE THE POWER OF SENSES TO GRAB ATTENTION

From our childhood, we are hardwired to believe in what we see. It goes without saying that visual graphics have always had a great impact on the human mind compared to reading texts. The concept of sensory marketing is not a new phenomenon. A striking website with the right combination of creativity and imagery is what's needed to carve up a niche and attract more customers.

Just imagine the website has captivated the attention of the customer in that moment when they are looking for just that right piece of information via an enticing, engaging, and informative website. This phenomenon is called the Zero Moment of Truth by Google. This is the moment where marketing happens, where information is gathered, and where consumers make their choices—choices that affect the success and failure of almost all brands around the world, irrespective of the industry in which a business operates.

In the eyes of customers, a website is a reflection of the organization. If a website looks cheap and is not user-friendly, this does not leave a good impression on website visitors. To convert traffic into sales leads, a high-quality website is critical, giving the consumer a glimpse of the how the business can satisfy their needs, how customers can receive services, and what makes the business different from competition.

THE IMPORTANCE OF THE LANDING PAGE

Often known as the lead capture page or Lander, the landing page for a brand serves as the linchpin to its offerings. This is where rubber meets the road. It is crunch time, and visitors to this page will either commit to a promotion or move on, so it is critical to optimize the landing page.

The landing page serves as a teaser of the brand and should stimulate the appetite of customers. Simply driving website visitors directly to a homepage is an ineffective way of converting prospects. A landing page offers a streamlined path that is designed to bring forth a specific response—a call to action *vis-à-vis* the visitor. The landing page is designed to serve the following purposes:

- Getting a web visitor to click in order to go to another page
- Getting a visitor to buy
- Getting a visitor to comment or give feedback
- Getting permission from a visitor so you can follow up by e-mail, phone, etc.

KEEP IT SIMPLE

When creating landing pages, it is important to keep them simple. The more complicated for website visitors, the lower the conversion rate.

USE INTERACTIVE GRAPHICS

There are only eight seconds to grab the attention of a website visitor; use images and videos whenever possible to describe the organization's product or service. This will not only make the landing page more interesting, but it will also improve the conversion rate.

Of course, a good web design is not all about the technical wizardry that goes on in its backend. An impressive website design that is visually appealing will automatically result in user engagement. As a result, visitors will spend more time on a website leading them to view business processes and offerings more carefully. To be successful, a website needs to

- be easy to navigate to information;
- represent an organization in its best light and look professional and trustworthy;
- be attractive and professional while reinforcing the brand message;
- be SEO friendly to improve page ranking on search engines;
- be regularly updated; and
- be interactive; it is important to infuse it with creative and interactive elements such as guest books, or e-mail forms to maintain consumers' interest and give them a reason to revisit.

ADDING META TAGS AND KEYWORDS

You are not ready to submit your website to search engines without meta tags, used by major search engines in their ranking algorithms. These tags not only improve search engine ranking but also display valuable information on search results.

While only a few meta tags play a direct role in site promotion, make use of other meta tags to provide useful information about the content on the organization's website. In addition to meta tags, keywords also act as a valuable tool in helping search engines index a website. When selecting keywords for a website, consider the following points:

- Do not overload web pages with keywords in order to influence a search engine. This can actually backfire, and the website might be penalized for keyword stuffing or spamming.
- Take some time to come up with keywords that appropriately describe your organization. Make sure that these keywords are used effectively in meta tags as well as web pages. It is also important to give a descriptive title to all web pages.
- The title displayed in the topmost bar of your browser as well as in the user's bookmark list not only helps the website gain a good search engine ranking but also helps website visitors orient themselves.

When determining the search engine ranking of a website, most search engines do not just consider keywords but also the quantity and quality of links on and to the website. So just how do you define quality links?

When a search query is submitted, search engines return with hundreds or even thousands of search results. The goal is to make the organization's website appear in the top search results. In simple words, attracting traffic needs good search engine rankings.

Search engines consider a number of factors when determining search engine rank, including where the website should appear in the search results. From the load speed to relevant keywords to quality back links, everything matters. However, one of the most important considerations is the quantity, quality, and relevance of the links on and to the website.

Also referred to as inbound links, back links are the web pages on the Internet that create a link back to a website. These links constitute an important part of algorithms for major search engines such as Google, Yahoo, and Bing. Not only do they help search engines find a website, they also serve to improve search engine rankings.

UNLEASHING THE WEB TO DRIVE THE SALES FUNNEL

A sales funnel can be described as a process through which customers move in order to buy something from an organization. In simple words, it is a graphical illustration of the flow through which target customers pass in order to reach their ultimate decision—purchasing a product or service.

A less-established brand will require a more thorough sales funnel in order to make customers trust the brand. At the end of the day, the goal is to maximize the flow of target prospects through various stages of the sales funnel in order to generate sales and, ultimately, profits.

Stage 1: Generate traffic to the website

The primary focus of a web-based marketing campaign is to drive traffic toward an organization's website, and this effort is enhanced by including content useful to prospective customers in the form of blogs, articles, downloadable resources, and so forth.

Organizations producing such content-rich websites understand that people need information in order to shape their opinions and attitudes. And nothing can beat the Internet for providing information, be it in the form of blogs, web pages, or articles.

While a good website is essential for success in today's wired world, it requires a large and enduring commitment that will certainly provide a good return on the investment of time, budget, and attention. It is essential to create content for the website in order to maintain its ranking on search engines.

Regularly updating the website with quality optimized content will retain or elevate rankings on search engines and attract more traffic. In other words, when more pages with optimized content are added, so are the chances of being found on search engines that are attracting more visitors.

In order to increase the user engagement and attract more visitors toward a website, it is very important to make sure that all web pages are properly linked together. Additionally, when search engines evaluate a website they often assess the number of quality links that connect to an organization's website and determine the ranking based on it. The more popular a website (having more quality links), the higher will be the search engine ranking.

Stage 2: Generate leads

By setting up, designing, and monitoring the website to maximize traffic to the site, the next stage of the Internet marketing sales funnel is generating leads. If a website successfully manages to grab the attention of its visitors, it is vital to keep them interested in order to move them forward through the sales funnel.

Another important thing to keep in mind is the concept of "lead nurturing," an approach of developing a relationship with immature prospects who may otherwise not continue through the sales funnel. Though prospects at this stage may not be ready to buy, lead nurturing and information about the prospect will be helpful in maintaining a relationship and bringing the prospect back when the timing and conditions are right.

Stage 3: Generate prospects

The next stage of the sales funnel is generating prospects. This is the middle of the funnel (MOFU) where target customers may be showing barriers to consumption. At this stage, the goal is to inspire trust and move toward a positive purchase decision. This stage is perhaps the most critical stage of the sales funnel, especially if the organization offers "high involvement" products or services (e.g., big-ticket items like automobiles, cruise-ship vacations, enrolling in an MBA program) purchased only after long and careful consideration. This stage will likely require a lot of work and attention to prospects and to the additional information they may require before making a buying decision.

Stage 4: Generate sales

The last stage of the sales funnel is the close, and the process results in a sale and the generation of revenue. It's critical to move the sale into a long-term relationship, where loyalty results in lower overall marketing costs and good word of mouth or referrals leverage the value of a satisfied and loyal customer.

THE MARKETING POWER OF SOCIAL MEDIA

Social media websites such as Facebook, Twitter, LinkedIn, and Instagram offer a great platform to grow a network, maximize brand visibility, and attract more visitors to your website. Organizations have realized the potential of social media in building a brand and are increasingly allocating more of their advertising budget to social media. The key is to inform people and direct them to the website for more information.

Social media is not just about creating a Facebook page or setting up a Twitter account. It requires serious efforts on the part of a business.

Once a profile has been set up on a social media website, the most important step is to retain followers and fans by posting interesting and informative content. There are tools to organize, coordinate, and simplify the process of updating multiple social media accounts, where posts can be automated across many social media sites and at predetermined times and dates. Online media and sharing facilitates you to upload and share various types of content, including videos, documents, and podcasts.

E-MAIL MARKETING

With e-mail marketing, it is very easy to connect with customers and for customers to share messages with their networks. And the more these customers spread the word, the more you experience growth in website traffic and activity.

In order to start building an e-mail list, invite contacts to the website and make it worth their while by providing helpful and useable content. The list can be used to create ongoing interest in order to engage and maintain online relationships; growing an e-mail list requires an exchange for something of value.

ETHICS AND REGULATORY ISSUES

Ethics in promotional activities is critical. Most common ethical violations are those marked by puffery and deception. Puffery is an exaggerated claim about the superiority of a product. Although puffery is legal, it may cause a company to lose its reputation with the public. Deception involves a company deliberately making promises that are not true. A consumer may have legal recourse for deception. An example of a deceptive practice that is illegal is bait and switch advertising: this is when a company advertises a product as on sale, and when the consumer arrives, that product is not available, but the company offers the customer another more expensive product as a substitute.

Another area of ethical debate is marketing to children and teenagers. This is particularly a concern when it comes to tobacco or alcoholic beverages. It is illegal for companies to target those who are legally unable to consume their products.

Other situations of ethical concern when it comes to marketing to children arise when a company such as a beverage company signs a contract with a school to supply their brand of beverages exclusively on the school campus. This is not an illegal practice, but it is controversial, as some feel that the school is being controlled by corporations that want children to become hooked on their products or become brand loyal.

MARKETING AS AN INVESTMENT

Successful organizations that become excellent in marketing know themselves, their customers, and what they offer that fills the customer's need. This requires an investment of time and money to accurately determine whether or not all three parts of the triangle fit together.

As an example, ABC Company is about eight years old and operates in the online professional services industry. The customer wants and needs this service. Most importantly, the customer is willing to pay for the service, and ABC Company is the only company occupying this space at this time. One would imagine that ABC Company is generating a strong and regular revenue stream. Unfortunately, ABC Company's CEO does not believe in investing in consistent marketing strategies and targeted marketing initiatives. Rather, the CEO pays low wages to inexperienced sales people who have no incentive or support to sell the service. Therefore, due to a lack of investment in marketing, the customer does not even know that ABC Company exists. The fallout of such poor strategic thinking could be any or all of the following: employees often are not paid in a month, morale plummets, and company reputation lags.

BECOMING A MARKETING ORGANIZATION: BE TRUE TO YOURSELF

As set forth in the preceding sections, marketing is the process of building a strategic plan. However, without buy-in from the organization as a whole, becoming a marketing organization is more challenging.

A marketing organization is a firm—regardless of industry, function, size, or region—in which all levels of the organization adhere to the same ideals and uniform methods for attaining customers. As an example, Southwest Airlines has created a marketing organization. They have three company policies:

1. Practice the Golden Rule. We have a choice every day and choose to make our employees our first customers and our passengers our second customers.
2. Help each other out.
3. Feel free to be yourself.

INTEGRATE, INTEGRATE, INTEGRATE

Southwest Airlines ensures that these messages, as well as any marketing message, are integrated throughout every part of the organization and in every point of contact with the customer—noting that the customer is both the Southwest employee as well as the ticket-purchasing passenger. This ability on Southwest's part to create a marketing organization—or a marketing culture—helps the company weather economic downturns and adverse industry trends.

Becoming a marketing organization also allows the entire team to understand the value of the firm's products to the customer and behave in a manner in which "selling" is a way of life.

For example, a consulting firm may have strategic consultants working on projects at the client's office. Because of this situation, the consultants are able to observe the client's business processes at every stage, and thus have an inside view of the needs of the client. This can create an upsell opportunity. *Upselling* is the process of adding a product or service to an existing project. For all marketers, gaining more share of an existing customer is a more effective overall marketing strategy than working hard to find more customers.

Customer or client loyalty is a much smarter long-term strategy, because satisfied customers become "salespeople" by attracting new customers.

Additionally, satisfied customers have trust and confidence in your firm's offerings and are more likely to buy more, buy more often, and, because of the lower marketing costs associated with existing customers, become more profitable. The most expensive customer to acquire is a new customer; the most cost-efficient customer is an existing one.

There are numerous ways to enhance marketing efforts and create buy-in on all levels:

- Communication: A firm may ensure that decisions are communicated quickly and honestly on all levels of the company so that employee questions, fears, and rumors do not erupt.
- Training: Training is important to ensure that every employee knows exactly what the firm does to generate revenue and what impact that individual has over that process. Ongoing training in customer service, at all levels of the organization, will add greatly to the effectiveness of the company's marketing strategy.
- Tools of the trade: People take action when empowered with the right tools to do so; therefore, it is important to create the tools to make each employee's job easier—whether it be a technological system, a brochure to distribute to customers, or the process to do his or her job with clarity.

STRATEGY

In a word, strategy is a bridge that connects a firm's internal environment with its external environment, leveraging its resources to adapt to, and benefit from, changes occurring in its external environment.

Strategy is also a decision-making process that transfers a long-term vision into day-to-day tactics to fulfill the long-term plan. Although often thought of only as something reflected in a business plan, strategy is rather a continual process of assessment, reassessment, and analysis, which constantly provides direction to the firm. Strategy can be compared to the captain on the bridge of a ship, who is constantly scanning both the horizon and the immediate surroundings and adjusting the course, possibly taking the ship in another direction if a storm appears on the horizon or if an object appears to obstruct the path.

POSITIONING AND STRATEGY

The position the firm fills in the marketplace is an integral part of the strategic process. Positioning can also be thought of as how the firm will stake a claim in a piece of the marketplace in a manner that will differentiate it from the competitor.

The key to sustainable strategy and positioning is an integrated marketing system. Competitive advantage comes from the ability to identify the firm's position, make strategic plans, and engage an entire integrated marketing system. All activities of the firm should fit together and compliment each other to produce a well-oiled machine, which creates differentiation in the customer's mind and competitive advantage.

Strategy involves all areas of the firm, from operations to finance to human resources. Choosing the right strategy for the right people for the right goals is challenging, yet it provides an overarching message for the entire organization. The strategy and message must then be communicated consistently and clearly throughout the firm for its effectiveness to take effect and produce a sustainable organization.

TACTICS

What is the difference between strategy and tactics? Strategy is the overall direction, the long-term mile markers, and/or the guiding force of how the organization moves forward, while tactics are the specific steps that are taken to implement the strategy. Thinking of the difference in another way, strategy tends to be focused on the long term and tactics take place in the short term, i.e., tactics are short term activities performed to pursue, and execute a long term strategy.

For example, ABC Company is a health and fitness center. Strategically, the firm leadership has decided to develop a center targeted at the thirty-to-sixty-five-year-old woman and create a comfortable environment in which she can exercise, lose weight, and learn more healthy life habits. The firm's strategic geographic positioning is to provide centers in suburban areas where the largest number of these women live.

The tactics used for carrying out this strategy include developing consistent messages and advertisements reflecting the mission of the firm and targeted to this market segment, hiring other women trainers so the women customers will be comfortable, and providing educational materials on health and fitness that are specific to the adult woman customer that will create a relationship between ABC Company and this market segment.

PEST ANALYSIS

Although easily forgotten by firms in developing a long-term strategy, a PEST analysis is an easy-to-remember acronym for analyzing the external environment and setting the stage for strategic planning. Also known as environmental scanning, the PEST analysis reviews the political, economic, sociological/demographic and technological environment of a market—whether emerging or existing—and provides a snapshot of the external situation that may impact an industry or the firms within that industry.

POLITICAL

Often considered more relevant when entering a foreign market, the political situation in any new or existing market is invaluable to study and understand.

Existing government policies and regulations can deter new entrants into an economy, particularly in underdeveloped or developing areas of the world, or can swiftly affect incumbents in an industry with new regulations and policies, which can have both positive and negative results.

For example, even though the Graham-Leach-Bliley Act in the 1990s in the United States repealed the New Deal–era Glass-Steagall Act and allowed some companies to expand their services, it also impacted those firms that had been operating solely because firms were not permitted to sell both institutional and investment services.

Likewise, the Sarbanes-Oxley Act of 2002 prohibited firms such as those in accounting and financial services from providing consulting and auditing services. Additionally, government policies can add extra expense to firms; for example, the HIPAA regulations of the late 1990s required health-care organizations and all related firms to protect patient information, which led to increased costs to these providers.

ECONOMIC

The economic health and welfare of a state, nation, or region also impacts the firm's decision-making process. If an area is healthy economically and the consumers in a region have the means or potential means for creating purchasing power, then a company may want to consider that area to sell its product or service.

SOCIOLOGICAL/DEMOGRAPHIC

In this part of an environmental scan, we look at trends and factors of the population of our market—for instance, societal attitudes or population shifts that represent either opportunities or threats to our overall strategy. Included in this portion of the analysis is perhaps the education level of the local market, both in terms of creating a workforce and a customer base for the firm.

If the levels are too low, then the cost of creating training programs for potential employees and educational marketing methods for potential customers should be taken into consideration. The aging of the Baby Boomer demographic has affected the strategies of many organizations; interestingly, AARP has responded recently by becoming more "hip" in its image as a way to woo Boomers who, prior to their arrival into AARP age range, have parodied its existence.

TECHNOLOGICAL

Technology refers not only to technology as it is thought of today, with computers and systems to manage business more effectively, but it also refers to the infrastructure necessary to support modern systems and processes. Certainly the diffusion of web-based technology has affected most organizations, giving even the smallest a global presence and a cost-effective way to reach millions of potential customers. Thus, the strategy of an organization may be affected by technological change, and the velocity of technology change also means this variable must be monitored constantly. Certain areas of the world—even in the United States—cannot support systems without great build-out expense and investment. A firm must look at the condition of the host country or region's communication, transportation, and power systems, as well as the cost of using those systems. If the condition and cost are adequate, then the quality of the end product or service and the reliability of consistently providing the firm's product or service to the end user/customer must be analyzed.

A MODEL FOR STRATEGIC THINKING: PORTER'S FIVE FORCES

In the 1970s, Harvard economist Michael Porter created the gold standard for how strategy is created and analyzed today. Referred to as Porter's Five Forces, this method analyzes the industry and competitive environment in which a firm operates. When developed correctly, the framework paints a picture of the current environment in which the firm competes, allowing the firm to see the big picture and, in turn, develop long-term strategies for the company that will lead to effective decision-making and sustainability.

Porter believes that an industry's potential profitability can be expressed as a function of these five forces and that one can therefore determine the potential success of a firm in that industry. Porter's Five Forces provide a model for reviewing the outside environment portion of the strategy bridge and for determining the attractiveness of a particular activity at a particular moment in time. This model can be used on any firm of any size in any location in any industry and can be utilized regularly to keep a constant eye on the market, the direction of the market, and the competitors coming and going within that market.

Here are the essential elements of Porter's analytical framework:

BARRIERS TO ENTRY

Barriers to entry, or the threat of new entrants, refers to forces that deter companies from entering a particular market. In general terms, one will hear such references as "…the barriers to entry in the telecommunications market are extremely high…" or "…the barriers to entry in the ice cream industry appear to be quite low…"

Barriers to entry are just as important for firms that are incumbents in an industry as for the newcomers. The barriers generally observed by Porter include economies of scale, product differentiation, capital requirements, cost disadvantage independent of size, access to distribution channels, and government policies (regulation).

ECONOMIES OF SCALE

This refers to the ability of a firm to mass-produce a product and therefore to sell to the customer at a lower price. A competitor that does not have the luxury or means to mass-produce would thus not be able to compete on price, but rather would be forced to find another way to differentiate itself from the competition to the consumer.

PRODUCT DIFFERENTIATION

Product differentiation is the method or tactics used by a firm to give its product a more recognized value than competitors' product(s). Brand identity is a powerful tool in creating value and therefore makes it difficult for a new entrant into the market to gain customer loyalty. For example, the leaders in the toothpaste market are Colgate and Crest. Customers tend to be loyal to their toothpaste brands, and it would require heavy expenditures to draw customers away from either of those brands. In addition to brand identity, advertising, first mover advantage (being first in an industry), and differences in products also foster loyalty to products and can easily make entering a market highly expensive.

CAPITAL REQUIREMENTS

This is the amount of money and investment necessary to enter a market. Not only does this reference the product differentiation and brand loyalty mentioned above, but it is also extremely important in an industry in which the infrastructure to produce the product requires large amounts of financial resources. Both telecommunications and aviation are examples of industries that require investment in machinery, technology, and so forth.

COST DISADVANTAGE

Independent of size, some industries have a high learning curve, whether that is scientific, technological, or experiential. In other cases, companies in a particular industry may have access to raw materials and lower prices based on history or relationships, favorable locations, or even the benefit of government subsidies. All of these factors can affect the ability of an up-and-comer to set up business, get access to capital, and even be profitable.

ACCESS TO DISTRIBUTION CHANNELS

Incumbents in an industry have relationships that may have been function-ing profitably for all parties for years. New entrants to that industry have the challenge of creating new relationships or even new and creative methods of distribution just to get their products to market and in front of the consumer. This may mean using price breaks, innovative marketing, and creative prod-uct differentiation. For a service industry, this may refer to selling relation-ships or even a location of the service or places in society.

For example, some law firms build relationships with clients and partners that are a result of years of networking and relationships. Business between the organizations goes back generations, and new law firms in the field must be creative in reaching the clients.

GOVERNMENT POLICIES (REGULATIONS)

The government has power over industries in the form of licenses, limits on access to raw materials, taxation, and even environmental regulation and standards.

THREAT OF SUBSTITUTE PRODUCTS OR SERVICES

A substitute to a product or service can be any other product or service that serves a similar function. Too often, firms underestimate the competitor by not realizing that the product the competitor sells may be a substitute for its own product or service. Many failed ventures during the "dot com bubble" had the misconceived notion that "we have no competition," when, in fact, there are always products or services that compete for a consumer or cus-tomer's budget.

The key to a substitute is that although it may not be the same product or service and although the competing products or services may not function in the same manner, the competing products meet the same customer need.

For example, sugar prices cannot go too high because sugar substitutes such as fructose or corn syrup can be used in various consumable products (beverages, clothes, etc.).

BARGAINING POWER OF SUPPLIERS

By controlling the quality or quantity of a product or service, a firm conducts its business, or by affecting the price, a supplier can have power over the firm and impact its ability to enter or function in a new market.

The ultimate power of a supplier comes down to the characteristics of the supplier group and the relative importance of sales. According to Porter, a supplier group is powerful—can affect a firm and possess control over the firm—if and when

- there are fewer suppliers than buyers;
- its product is unique or differentiated;
- the buyer group is fairly small; and
- it has created high switching costs.

SWITCHING COSTS

These costs are incurred when a customer switches from one supplier/product/service to another. This does not occur with every kind of product or service. For example, when switching from one deodorant to another, the consumer may not experience a switching cost. However, for a company to switch from one office software provider to another, the costs may be substantial and involve human resources, time, training, and so on.

BARGAINING POWER OF CONSUMERS/BUYERS

Just as the supplier has power in the competition and market wars, the customer has power. Customers can force down prices, demand more service or better quality, and even pit competitors against one another. As with most situations, when buyers form groups, they become powerful and will remain powerful if and when

- they purchase in volume. A prime example is Walmart or Costco. Not only can the customer purchase in volume, but Walmart can purchase in large volume from the supplier, forcing down prices for the end consumer.
- the product is undifferentiated, and the alternatives for the buyer increase.
- the product that they purchase forms a component of the product they produce.
- switching costs are low.
- they can purchase upfront.
- they can integrate backward.

RIVALRY AMONG COMPETITORS

All four of the above parts—barriers to entry, bargaining power of buyers, bargaining power of suppliers, and the threat of substitutes—create rivalry among competitors. Analyzing all of these areas provides a platform for studying the competition in the firm's market space.

COMPETITIVE ADVANTAGE AND THE BASIS FOR COMPETING

Once the firm knows who the competitors are and what they do, it needs to carefully identify and document who it is. This is called creating a competitive advantage. A competitive advantage is created through differentiation, and differentiation is created through branding and imaging.

Any time a customer asks for a product by name, there is evidence of differentiation. Although theoretically simple, creating differentiation through brand and image is not as simple as it sounds. It is a process of identifying the firm's strengths, weaknesses, limitations, and hurdles, followed by creating a brand that is identified by logos, taglines, color schemes, and all those additional elements that create a visual or recognizable memory of the firm. The competitive advantage of a product or service also depends heavily on variables, such as the level of sophistication of the product, prior experience with that product or service in a certain country or part of a country, and the types of distribution channels available.

COSTS AND RISKS

Creating competitive advantage may require a high level of cost and risk to the organization. Often, an organization will create a branding strategy that "pushes the envelope" and increases risk both in time and money. However, the brand image that is created is so strong that the customer immediately responds positively. It is imperative that the brand or image created be aligned with the firm's strategic initiatives and goals.

CREATING A PERCEIVED VALUE

There are two packages of cheese; both are produced at the same factory. One is sold at the supermarket for $3.50 and carries a brand name. The other package of cheese carries a generic brand and sells for $2.00 before the store gives a "VIP card" (frequent shopper) discount. It is the exact same cheese with different labels. However, millions of Americans buy Kraft over the store brand because it is a brand they can trust. This is what is referred to as *perceived value.* The customer has no idea that the cheese comes from the same plant, has the same ingredients, and is probably even packaged at the same location. It is even possible that the same truck delivered both cheeses to the grocery store. The value is not in the cheese, but in the trust that the customer places in a company with which he or she can identify.

THE SWOT ANALYSIS

Once the competition and the industry have been assessed, an organization may wish to perform a SWOT analysis. SWOT stands for Strengths,

Weaknesses, Opportunities, and Threats. The strengths and weaknesses are internal factors, whereas opportunities and threats are external factors. A SWOT analysis can be as high-level or detailed as necessary to understand and bring to light the challenges and next steps for the firm in creating strategic initiatives.

To fully understand the firm's competitors and the competitive environment, it is imperative the firm compare its SWOT to its competition's SWOT. Most business leaders will want to ensure that a SWOT analysis is performed at regular intervals and that input on the SWOT is gathered from many areas of the organization as well as from the customer.

PERFORMING A COMPETITIVE ANALYSIS: KNOWING THE COMPETITION INSIDE AND OUT

Once the organization's internal strengths and weaknesses are realized and the external opportunities and threats are identified, it is important to turn next to a similar process of evaluating the competition. Competitor evaluation not only gives more insight into the strategies and goals of the competition but also provides a bird's-eye view of the trends and future of the industry in which the firm operates.

Step 1: Identify the competition
To analyze the competitive landscape, it is necessary to make a list of those competitors that compete directly or indirectly with the firm's product or service by filling the same need to the customer. The need that is fulfilled by a product or service is not necessarily the obvious. For example, in the case of a beauty salon, the customer need is not a haircut but rather the need to look good and feel happy and attractive.

Step 2: Identify the competitors' strategies
Analyzing the competitors' strategies provides the firm an indication of current trends in the marketplace. This helps the firm determine how to approach the customer.

Step 3: Determine the competitors' objectives and goals

This step may also be referred to as determining "competition's internal balance." The key to properly assessing the competitor is to know where its value system lies. Because each competitor is different, it will place various levels of importance on technology, quality, cost, market share, and mission. Understanding the competition's objectives can help the firm identify those things that may differentiate it from the rest of the pack.

Step 4: Identifying competitor SWOT

In this step, it is not only important to assess each competitors' strengths and weaknesses, just as the organization performed on itself, but it is also valuable to recognize those opportunities and threats that may be present for the competition. Identifying the competition's strengths and weaknesses allows the organization to identify and assess future moves and initiatives that could affect both the industry and the organization, while identifying the opportunities and threats will give the idea of the kinds of outside forces that could impact the competition and therefore attack the organization.

Step 5: Estimate the competitors' reaction patterns

Some competitors react quickly to events in the marketplace, whereas other competitors take a different approach and react only to selective events in the marketplace. Others are laid-back and react slowly, while others don't show a pattern of reaction at all. Looking at these behaviors provides the firm a better understanding of what may occur in an industry if the firm takes certain actions or implements certain initiatives.

Step 6: Select the competitors to attack and avoid

Some competitors are such large financial powerhouses that it may not be financially feasible to attack them. Some merely put up the front or the image that they cannot be attacked. It is in this step that it is valuable to the organization to know the competitors for which an attack strategy would be profitable and those for which avoidance would be the best policy. Identifying the weak versus the strong competitors will allow the organization to make efficient decisions.

Step 7: Create a positioning map

To create a visual understanding of the entire competitive landscape, it is helpful to create a positioning map to provide a visual representation of the firm's position compared to the competition.

Competition provides the organization the opportunity to look into the future. Once all of the information is gathered, an organization can imagine the competitor's next move and either do the same if the market supports it or take a different route, cutting the competition off "at the pass." For example, the home improvement stores Home Depot and Lowe's are often within minutes of each other or even right across the street. Generally, one store decides to move into an area before the other, and the other watches and sets up shop nearby. Competition creates a sense of urgency and often increases sales for all the competitors who are willing to put up a fight. Once the firm's competition is known and understood, the next opportunity for the organization is to "go deeper," by implementing competitive intelligence.

COMPETITIVE INTELLIGENCE: WHAT CAN YOUR COMPETITION DO FOR YOU?

Competitive intelligence, also referred to as business intelligence, is often seen as the business world's secret agent 007. Although no spy planes or pinpoint cameras are used, competitive intelligence (CI) is, according to the Society for Competitive Intelligence Professionals:

> a systematic and ethical program for gathering, analyzing, and managing external information that can affect (the organization's) plans, decisions, and operations. Specifically, (CI) is the legal collection and analysis of information regarding

the capabilities, vulnerabilities, and intentions of business competitors, conducted by using information databases and other "open sources" and through ethical inquiry.

In other words, CI is the company's radar.

Organizations use CI for any number of reasons, from assessing a competitor's strategies, to defining the competitive landscape, to discovering and assessing trends in the industry. It is also used for identifying new opportunities that may not have surfaced earlier in the competitive analysis process.

Unlike market research, CI is more forward-looking; CI is also not considered industrial espionage because it is legal. CI is a systematic and timely process for understanding the current competitive environment. CI can provide a decision-maker a more complete picture of the decisions that need to be made to retain the organization's competitive advantage.

Further, CI is valuable because it can help both decrease the possibility for risk and help the organization avoid unnecessary or additional costs. In terms of savings, it can increase revenues and save time, which translates into cost savings. CI also provides information for innovation, product development, and targeted marketing by validating trends, clarifying events, and providing discovery and insightful information.

Because any effective strategic marketing plan requires that an organization keep close track of competitors' plans and actions, there are a number of ways that CI can be done. To find out information about the competition, the following are a few obvious or not-so-obvious places where information about the competition can be found:

- **Annual reports.** Annual reports are an obvious and easily accessible way to learn how a competitor is revealing itself to shareholders for publicly held companies.

- *Press releases.* Most firms distribute press releases to generate public relations. Often, the firm will post these on its website. It is advisable to review the press releases over a few months' time to get a big picture view of where the competitor's strategy is heading.
- *Trade magazines.* Trade magazines provide an up-to-date and in-depth analysis of the industry and where that industry appears to be headed.
- *Vendors/partners/customers.* Another source of solid competitor information is the patterns of vendors, partners, and customers.
- *Salespeople.* Salespeople are often very willing to talk about their companies and provide information that provides insight into the direction the competition is heading.
- *Networking.* In the process of creating a network for generating business for the firm, it is possible to hear about the activity of the competition merely through observing the activities or events the senior leadership attends.
- Often local, regional, and national news sources track the activities of local private companies and have access to articles on websites and even search engines.
- *10-Ks and 10-Qs.* A public company's SEC filings are especially helpful when considered as an evolving story over a period of years.
- *External research or professional organizations.* Often the best place to find information about a company is an event at which representatives of the company have been asked to speak. This may be at any professional organization's monthly meetings or annual conference. In addition, there are plenty of online resources, including organizations such as Hoovers or Dun & Bradstreet, that can help if time or money is a limitation.
- *The Internet.* Search engines can be an invaluable source of information. For example, once the names of the competitors' senior management teams are available, it is possible to plug a name into a search engine and reveal a host of information.

SUMMARY

Many methods are used by marketers to attract customers to their brands and products. A successful integrated marketing campaign will consist of a consistent message that is brought to the target audience through different mediums of the marketing mix. Advertising and promotional messages should be consistent and repeated often in order to create a clear image in the mind of consumers. Ideally, these promotional efforts will result in influencing consumers to either try new products, switch from their preferred products, or purchase more products from a company or brand. The end goal of all promotional efforts is to increase the company's product sales and profits through gaining or taking market share.

An organization's strategic goals are based on both internal and external knowledge, insight, and in-depth analysis. Without a strategic plan, resources are spent on events, activities, and functions that may not generate revenue. To make the most of each dollar earned by the firm, all functions must work together to create a well-oiled machine. The marketing plan, which is based on a full understanding of the market, the firm, and the customer needs, dovetails directly with the strategic plan to provide a roadmap for the firm. This roadmap is the ultimate tool for guiding leaders toward making decisions that will result in sustainable growth for the company.

Chapter 10

COMMUNICATIONS AND PRESENTATIONS

P resentations can range from a short talk before a small group of acquaintances or colleagues to a lengthy speech to a group of strangers. No matter the audience or the setting, formal or informal, small or large, the best presentations leave the audience informed, interested, and wanting to know more about the subject matter. A good indicator of a good presentation is when, after the presentation, members of the audience follow up with insightful comments and questions for the presenter. A bad presentation, on the other hand, leaves the audience confused or bored and often makes them wonder why they wasted their time. A poor quality presentation detracts from the importance of the subject matter and can be detrimental to the reputation of the presenter.

In addition to length and format, presentations can also vary in purpose. The main purpose of a presentation is to communicate ideas and information as well as to serve as persuasion, instruction, inspiration, and/or entertainment.

Regardless of length, format, or purpose, presentations are an important and useful tool in all aspects of business. All too often, an associate is assigned the task of "giving a presentation" and then left to do so without any coaching or advice. No wonder so many individuals list public speaking as their greatest fear.

TO PRESENT OR NOT TO PRESENT

Assuming the decision is made to make a presentation, it's important to think about its time commitment, inasmuch as preparing for any presentation takes time. A rough estimate for an effective presentation is that it takes thirty to sixty minutes of preparation for each minute of delivery. Is there enough focused time prior to the presentation to properly prepare? In addition, the presenter needs to look inside to ask whether or not there's enough interest, energy, and knowledge about the subject matter to deliver an effective and enthusiastic presentation. If the answer to either of these questions is a clear no, a would-be presenter should seriously consider turning down the offer to present.

BEFORE THE PRESENTATION

DEFINE THE PARAMETERS

Knowing the parameters beforehand will limit uncertainties and surprises and will allow the presenter to be better prepared to deliver a targeted, informative, and interesting presentation. The most important parameters are topic and theme, time, program, preservation, audience, space, and questions. Some of these parameters can be determined prior to the presentation. More than likely one or two of the later ones will change slightly by the day of the presentation. It is important to redefine the parameters shortly before the presentation in order to make sure that none of the changes will dramatically affect your presentation.

TOPIC, THEME, AND TIME

What will the presentation be about? What will be the message and point of view? What amount of time has been allocated to the presentation? Though the time to fill with a presentation may seem daunting, once the presentation process is underway, the amount of time will seem to be less troublesome, and in fact, by the time the presentation has been fully prepared, reducing the amount of content is often the challenge.

PROGRAM

Will there be other speakers presenting? How will the information in the presentation compare or contrast with the topics covered by other speakers? What is the order of the presentations? What is the theme of the conference, meeting, or event?

MEDIA FOR CAPTURING THE PRESENTATION

In this digital era where video recorders, smartphones, and GoPros are simple and inexpensive, it's relatively easy to make recorded presentations available for future viewing or public consumption; this also presents a good opportunity to review and critique a presentation for improvement or adaptation in the future.

AUDIENCE

The profile of the audience is critical in presentations. Giving a talk about trees to a group of executives in the forestry industry would be significantly different from giving the same talk to the members of an environmental group. Research the audience beforehand. What is their background, and how knowledgeable are they about the subject matter? What is the educational level or place in the hierarchy of the organization or profession? What are they expecting from the presentation? Are they expecting to be informed, amused, or challenged? How big is the audience? The size of the group will affect the "vibe" of the room and the manner by which the presentation is delivered.

PLACE

Often dictated by the size of the audience, another question will be about where the presentation is going to take place. How are the acoustics of the space? What audio-video resources are available at this location? In today's presentation environment, the on-site technology will likely vary from location to location, and most presenters find their presentations to be attractors of "Murphy's Law" (of presentations!). Irrespective of the time and energy spent on preparation, technology gaffes are presentation killers, compromising the professionalism of even the most well-planned presentation. Whenever possible, arrive at the venue and the presentation room well ahead of the time for the presentation for a tech check—a good antidote to Murphy's Law anxiety. Another factor in the physical dynamics of the presentation will be the layout of the room and the placement of the presenter in relation to the audience. Will it be theater style, with the presenter on a stage or in front of the audience sitting in rows, or will it be seminar style with the audience seated at tables arranged in a U formation or a modified theater style, with the tables forming rows?

QUESTIONS AND ANSWERS

Often, the quality of post-presentation questions is a good indicator of the quality and interest level of the presentation. If the format provides for post-presentation questions or discussion, will there be a moderator to take questions, or will the presenter be expected to handle them? If there are several presenters, will questions be taken at the end of each presentation or after all the presenters have spoken?

PURPOSE

Knowing the topic and theme is obviously important in delivering an effective presentation. Knowing the *why* for a presentation, however, is equally important. Generally, there are four common purposes for a presentation:

1. *Persuasion* is a method for bringing an audience around to the presenter's point of view.
2. *Instruction* is used to share basic information about a topic.
3. *Inspiration* is effective when used during a change of process, procedure, or direction.

4.   ***Entertainment*** presents a diversion and lightens the mood.

Often these purposes are used to varying degrees in a presentation. The important point is to take a moment to think about what purpose is the most important and effective for the presentation and the audience. To help determine the purpose of a presentation, ask what is desired for people in the audience to do as a result of experiencing the presentation.

KEYS TO AN EFFECTIVE DELIVERY

One of the most important keys to a successful presentation is eye contact. With a written draft in hand, some presenters will keep their eyes glued to the printed page and neglect to make eye contact with their audience. Very formal presentations, or speaking to the press, require the presenter to stick to the exact words of the draft. Most other presentations are well served by a more spontaneous and original approach involving more eye contact with the audience, in which it is useful to identify key words and phrases in the draft and use these as prompts during the presentation delivery.

Step away from any form of a script and rehearse the presentation using these prompts. What do these key words and phrases convey? How do they fit into the presentation as a whole? Transfer these prompts to index cards and practice giving your presentation using these cards. Work toward linking these prompts together in your mind and using fewer and fewer of the cards. Continue practicing this process.

PRESENTATION AIDS

A variety of aids can be used to support a presentation's topic, theme, and purpose, including high-quality computer-generated graphics and multi digital media. Poor graphics, on the other hand, detract from it the presentation instead of supporting it by drawing the audience's attention away from the presenter.

An important principle is to use presentation aids to *support* the presentation and enhance (rather than replace) the connection between the audience and the presenter. These should be used to either summarize or add value to a specific point in the presentation, and they should

- flow with the script. Do the aids fit smoothly together with the topic, theme, and purpose of the presentation?
- be appropriate for the size and type of audience and the venue where the presentation is taking place.
- be clear, readable, and consistent from all places in the room where the presentation is to take place.

Make sure to have a printed copy of any of your visual presentation aids in case there are problems with technology; a printed version of the presentation is a critical safety net that's saved many presentations when the technology demons have their way.

WHAT'S THE POINT OF POWERPOINT?

Advances in technology have increased the percentage of information received visually. This has been especially true since Microsoft's PowerPoint dramatically changed the nature of presentations. Some people are now surprised if they attend a presentation and PowerPoint is not part of the program; however, many look forward to a PowerPoint presentation as they would look forward to a root canal. A dark room, a blue background with white lettering, and the audience struggles to stay awake and wonders what all that information was about that was flashed up on the screen only minutes ago.

PowerPoint is not a required element of a presentation, but it can be a useful tool. Remember, it's not the slides themselves that are the problem so much as it is the content of the slides and how well the presenter uses them.

One way to counter PowerPoint's problems is to focus on basics rather than on animation, clip art, video clips, and colorful backgrounds. The more complex a presentation, the more likely it will upstage the presenter. To keep slides visually simple, limit six words to one line and five lines to a slide. Also, use no more than three colors per slide.

PowerPoint should be used to provide a map of what the presenter will be talking about and to help provide context for the rest of the presentation. Don't use PowerPoint as a surrogate for your speech. PowerPoint is not a teleprompter. In fact, putting less material on a slide can provide a unique opportunity for discussion.

When working with PowerPoint, make sure the presenter knows the technology well, and use the Notes view of PowerPoint to write out what to say in the presentation. This will serve as a valuable check in making sure that what is shown on the slide directly relates to what the presenter is saying. In addition, it preserves a more detailed copy of the presentation to share with others or to review at a later date.

Minimize the number of slides used in a presentation. The fewer slides, the better. If there is additional material that needs to be shared, use handouts. Good presenters learn to use the B key, which will black out the screen, giving the audience a chance to shift their focus away from the screen and back to the most important part of the presentation: the presenter.

THE SPEAKER'S PODIUM AND ITS USE

A podium has always been a central fixture of lecture halls and auditoriums. If there is a podium in the room, a presenter will often be drawn to it like a magnet. This is not always for the best.

Although a podium can provide a sense of authority and a convenient place to rest the presenter's water glass, it can also serve as a barrier and hinder efforts to connect with an audience. If a podium is present and there is a convener for the meeting, ask where they expect presenters to deliver their presentations and think about the size and nature of the audience. With a smaller, less formal group, it's a good idea to step away from the podium to develop personal and individual relationships with audience members. With a larger, more formal audience, a podium can serve as a means to minimize stage fright and help the audience focus on the presenter.

SPEAKING ATTIRE

With all the thought a presenter is likely to have put into preparing for the presentation, it is possible that what to wear may be sidelined until the last minute. The most important thing to keep in mind is that choice of attire should not detract from the message being delivered. Dressing conservatively and neatly will convey professionalism of a presentation, and, of course, is the cell phone turned off?

CLOTHING DOS

- Always look professional
- Dress for the audience, the circumstance, and the corporate culture
- Wear clothes that fit
- Make sure clothes are pressed
- Keep jackets buttoned (formal)
- Err on the side of conservative
- Keep hair neat and trimmed
- Wear shirt with a simple collar and cuffs
- Keep watches formal but simple

CLOTHING DON'TS

- Clothes that talk louder than the presenter

- Clothing that no longer fits
- Wrinkled clothing
- Hairstyle that requires continual adjustment
- ID badges when presenting
- Busy patterns
- Jewelry that's distracting

POST-PRESENTATION CONSIDERATIONS

After a presentation, the script and visual aids often end up in a folder casually tossed and forgotten on a desk. It is time to get on with other things, and if the presenter needs to deliver the presentation again, it's usually simply recovered and used again. This approach is a mistake and wastes a valuable opportunity to take advantage of conducting an assessment of the presentation. Even letting a couple of days pass before reviewing the presentation will result in forgotten but valuable learning points.

If the presenter is fortunate enough to obtain a video recording of the presentation, it will be very useful to examine presentation style and effectiveness; multiple viewings are needed to fully capture the dynamics of a presentation. Each successive viewing will uncover new areas for improvement or enhancement.

SUMMARY

Presentations are an essential tool for leaders of today's organizations who find they are spending more and more time preparing for presentations and communicating their ideas with colleagues, customers, investors, and other stakeholders. It is essential that managers consider these presentation opportunities as important to advancing the organization's purpose and in achieving its goals and objectives.

Section IV

SYSTEMS AND PROCESSES

Chapter 11

❋   ❋   ❋

PROJECT MANAGEMENT

In this chapter, we will explore a concept and practice that has grown in importance as organizations have become more complex and are continuously evolving and implementing new ideas, products, and services or seeking to improve existing ones. An organization will create a project as a way to focus resources on an opportunity or issue and to serve as a way of effectively organizing its efforts to achieve a specific goal or objective. In a small firm, practice, or business, a *project* may be the installation of a new accounting software system or the introduction of a new product or service. In large, complex organizations, several projects may be in play at the same time, with some midlevel managers whose only responsibility is the management of a stream of these short-term assignments. In the dynamic nature of today's organizational environment, project management is an important concept and tool to understand and effectively implement.

According to the Project Management Institute (PMI), 74 percent of all projects fail. The projects can fail from a processes standpoint (initiation, planning, executing, controlling, or closing) or they can fail from a weakness in project dynamics (scope, time cost management, quality management, human resources management, communications, or risk). Project management covers a wide range of topics and issues and is defined as the application of knowledge, skills, tools, and techniques to a broad range of activities to reach a predetermined goal or objective.

It may also be concluded that a lot of projects fail from not having a skilled and experienced project manager to manage the process. This hole is quickly being filled, however, as companies recognize that successfully managed projects increase productivity, yield a greater return on investment, increase profits, and improve customer service.

But project management isn't new. Project management coordination and planning skills have been used for centuries—even as far back as the Roman Empire. Project management usually deals with the same elemental challenges: incomplete project specifications and scope definition, insufficient labor, unforeseen challenges, or unsure funding. The role and job title of the person responsible for managing these elements, however, the project manager, was not recognized until the twentieth century.

Another reason for the importance of the role of a project manager is the increasing rate of change in the workplace. Project management skills transcend corporations and industries; with change happening at such rapid rates, whether in technology, business, or construction, project managers are increasingly in demand.

STAFFING AND LEADING PROJECT TEAMS

It is important for all project participants to understand the process of project management. As project-based change increases, every project participant, from part-time team member to executive sponsor, will be more effective in their role if they understand the process of project management.

The *team* in project management is probably the most critical ingredient of the whole process. It is the responsibility of the project manager to motivate and guide the team to complete the project at hand. This may oblige the

PM to administer a variety of management techniques to develop a cohesive group. Change in the process must also be aptly managed. Managing the execution of the project requires being constantly aware of the project deliverables, objectives, schedule, costs, and quality. Monitoring all of this will allow the PM to quickly assess when the work of the team is deviating from the original plan and bring the team back on track.

Project managers have a large task. They must be able to define and manage quality throughout the project. They must be able to accurately determine the human resource requirements and be able to manage them. PMs must know how to develop and manage project planning and costs using the techniques discussed in this example. They must be effective communicators with all stakeholders—senior management, team members, clients, outsourced resources, and so forth—and they need to be familiar with the supply and contract management techniques.

In an effort to communicate effectively, the project team should make responsibility or task assignments and deadlines very clear from the beginning. They need to emphasize, again, the importance of communicating with all of the stakeholders: the managers and clients throughout the execution of the project. Expectations should be stated and effectively managed throughout the process so that surprises or disappointments are kept to an absolute minimum. It is also important that at the completion of the project, it is properly closed out.

PROJECT SCOPE AND THE WORK BREAKDOWN STRUCTURE

Let's begin with a discussion of the vocabulary and processes that encompass project management. The project scope involves subdividing the major project deliverables into smaller, more manageable components. Often this includes the work breakdown structure (or WBS). The project scope is a deliverable-oriented grouping of project elements that define the total scope of the project. The WBS is almost like a giant task list of what needs to get done to successfully complete the project. It is often used to help confirm a common understanding of what the project scope is. It has the ability to transform one large, unique, and sometimes mystifying job into many smaller, more manageable tasks.

The WBS helps to define deliverables and figure out the tasks that need to get done. The WBS is also a useful tool to help monitor the progress, verify the schedule estimates, and build project teams necessary to complete the project. It lists the tasks that need to get done in a prioritized, hierarchical structure in relation to what needs to get done in the overall project. Each task should be specific enough to be able to put a person's name next to it that will be able to execute the given activity.

Some of the items on the list will be open-ended tasks. Open-ended tasks include activities that we are familiar with but that don't have a specific deliverable or hard product being produced as a result. Examples of open-ended activities that might appear in a WBS are things such as research, perform analysis, or interview. Open-ended activities are another type of task that might be on the list to perform but need more clarification. Open-ended activities include listing things such as database, but what does that really mean? Does it mean sort the database? Clean the database? Load the database? Test the database? It's clear that just putting the word *database* on the list could refer to numerous activities; it is important that an activity is included. Therefore, a greater level of detail about the task needs to be achieved.

The WBS should include a plan for the project and output quality. Be sure to take the time necessary to get the quality high enough to meet expectations. It is cheaper to design and produce a product correctly the first time than it is to go in after development is in process and fix it. Steve McConnell, in his book *Rapid Development,* notes:

> If a defect caused by incorrect requirements is fixed in the construction or maintenance phase, it can cost 50 to 200 times as much to

fix as it would have in the requirements phase. Each hour spent on quality assurance activities such as design review saves 3 to 10 hours on downstream costs.

Product scope and project scope have different qualities. The product scope can remain constant throughout the process of the project, while the project scope can change and evolve and expand. The project may also focus on the creation and delivery of a service. If there is no detailed product description, then creating one should be the sole deliverable for a project. Defining what the project constraints are—costs, schedule, resources, material, and so forth—won't have any meaning unless the product specification is complete. This makes sense because if the project team doesn't have a clear idea of the product specification, they don't know what they're building or what they're working toward.

PROJECT DELIVERABLES AND OUTCOMES

Given that a product scope is understood, then, it is important to define the deliverables. What is being produced? Is it a product? A service? A new design? Fixing an old problem? It is critical that the team know what they are working toward, and it helps to create boundaries and focus the team on the outcome.

Deliverables can be both end deliverables and also intermediate deliverables. The end deliverable is what the final outcome of the project is expected to be. The intermediate deliverables are the small pieces of the puzzle that help the team get there. An intermediate deliverable, for example, could be the creation and description of a target market, when the end deliverable is the mass media advertising campaign for a product or service.

Setting project objectives is critical. They serve as quantifiable criteria that must be met in order for the project to be deemed successful. Project objectives should be specific and measurable so that they can provide the basis for agreement on the project. Measurability provides supporting detail that may be necessary to make a strong case for a particular outcome.

PROJECT SCOPE MANAGEMENT PLAN

When the product scope is understood, a product scope management plan needs to be created. The product scope management plan describes how the project scope will be managed and, therefore, any changes in scope will be integrated into the project. It also serves as an assessment of the anticipated stability of the project scope. In other words, it documents the characteristics of the product or service that the project was undertaken to create. The project scope management plan begins at initiation of the project and moves through scope planning, scope definition, scope verification, and scope change control (should this be needed).

SCOPING AND SETTING PROJECT BOUNDARIES

The initiation phase includes beginning with the scope's statement. The scope statement serves to put some boundaries on the project and keeps the scope from increasing as you delve into the meat of the project, which is a common phenomenon. The scope statement should describe the major activities of the project so clearly that it can be used to assess if extra work is necessary as the project process gets going. More simply, it serves to detail out exactly what has been agreed to from the beginning. It is understood that changes in the project scope require changes in the cost, schedule, and resource projections as these assumptions are made during the project planning and scope writing. Additionally, the scope statement can be used to help define where the project's placement is in a larger picture. This is the ideal place to clarify the relationship of this project to other projects in the total product development effort.

Another consideration in the initiation phase is the overall strategic plan of the organization. All projects should be supportive of the performing organization's goals, and having a strategic plan helps to make this possible. The project selection criteria are also very important to clarify in this phase. This is a good time to look at historical information and look to the results of previous project selection and performance.

The elements included in the initiation phase may include creating a project charter. The project charter is the product description and needs of the business addressed by the project. Identifying and assigning the project manager should also be one of the results of the initial phase. It is also important during this phase to identify constraints that will limit the project team's options and also identify the assumptions. The assumptions can include factors that will be considered true, real, or certain during the planning process and which will be more rigorously examined in the risk analysis phase of project planning.

The scope planning phase includes the scope statement (including the scope justification, project product description, project deliverables, project objectives, and the supporting detail).

When the major project deliverables are subdivided into small, more manageable components, the phase is called scope definition. The scope definition phase is also where you'll see the creation of the WBS.

The scope verification portion of the system is what may be used to determine if the job is complete. The process can actually proceed as soon as a deliverable is complete and can be measured, examined, and tested. Once verification is attained, you can move on to the next component of the project.

After formal acceptance of the scope (scope verification), scope change control takes place. It is likely that changes will occur after a project is underway. This phase influences factors that create scope changes to ensure that the changes being made are beneficial. A change control system will include the following steps:

- Recognizing that a change is needed
- Reviewing all requested changes
- Ensuring that any change is beneficial
- Evaluating the benefits of the requested change
- Identifying alternatives that would achieve the same result
- Identifying all impacted tasks
- Analyzing these impacts and how they affect project performance in terms of time, money, and scope
- Approving or rejecting the request
- Communicating the approved changes to all stakeholders
- Changing the baselines for performance monitoring
- Updating the project scope definition
- Implementing the change
- Documenting the change

It is critical that all changes get documented by the client prior to the change taking place. The agreement should not only detail what changes need to take place, but also how the change will occur and what the impact of the change will be on the overall scope.

PROJECT SCHEDULING

In order to modify for things such as scope changes, we need to be sure that there is a solid project schedule in place. The project scheduling process needs to include the activity definition, activity sequencing, activity duration estimating, schedule development, and the schedule control.

Examples of the primary tools used for project scheduling are Gantt Charts, CPM (Critical Path Method), and PERT (Program Evaluation and Review Technique). Critical Path Method and PERT are powerful tools that help you to schedule and manage complex projects. They were developed in the 1950s to control large defense projects and have been used routinely since then.

Gantt charts are simply a visual look at the major activities involved in a project, arranged so that the viewer will see the time-based relationships of the component parts of the project.

The CPM method helps you to plan out all tasks that must be completed as part of a project, and it acts as a basis both for preparation of a schedule and of resource planning. When managing a project, this tool can help monitor the achievement of project goals to date. It also helps to see where to take action to put a project back on track if it has fallen from its course. The CPM is useful because it

- identifies tasks that must be completed on time for the whole project to be completed on time;
- identifies which tasks can be delayed, if necessary, if resources need to be allocated somewhere else to catch up on missed tasks; and
- helps to identify the minimum length of time needed to complete the project.

PERT is a variation on Critical Path Analysis that takes a slightly more skeptical view of time estimates made for each project stage. To use it, estimate the shortest possible time each activity will take, the most likely length of time, and the longest time that might be taken if the activity takes longer than expected.

Project Scheduling essentially takes the definition of what the project is and breaks it down into smaller, more manageable tasks. It also identifies the relationships of each of the tasks to the other tasks. It illuminates in complete detail the actions that need to take place in order for the project to get accomplished. It then ensures the necessary order by using information about the activity duration as well as any external constraints that might exist. Finally, the project schedule ensures that the deadlines are met given the identified constraints, such as labor, materials, and other resources.

PROJECT BUDGETING

The next step is figuring out the project budget. Project budget estimates can be derived by using a variety of techniques ranging from pure estimation based on experience and knowledge to complicated financial models. An accurate, detailed, cost estimate is necessary to a project as soon as the project concept gets approval. The cost estimate created will become the standard for keeping the project costs in line and can be used by the client, the management team, the project manager, and the project management team.

A detailed and accurate budget also helps forecast the project funding needed and timing for the funds. As the project progresses, cost information will also be used to help control the project, monitor the progress, identify potential problems, and help to find solutions.

The calculation of the budget isn't what's difficult. The trick is getting those numbers as accurate as possible before the expenses have been incurred. The source of data for the budget is the most time-consuming part of the budgeting process.

In developing the budget, the first thing to think about is the internal labor costs. One of the biggest oversights of the budgeting process is leaving out the cost of internal staff in the project budget. This can be derived by using the detailed planning model to figure out how much of each person's time is going to be needed to get the job done. Then use the "burdened" labor rate. This rate is calculated by taking the average cost of an employee to the firm. It includes the costs for wages, benefits, and overhead. Most company finance departments keep this established rate on record, and it is not necessary to calculate and recalculate it from the project manager's point of view.

Getting an accurate cost for internal equipment used can be more complicated. If purchasing and using equipment for a single project, it is fairly straightforward to add up the cost of each and add it to the budget. If the project will be using equipment that gets used on multiple projects, a unit cost approach can help estimate how much of the equipment will be used for a specific project. One way to do this is to spread the cost over the time period of the expected use. Is it expected to use the equipment on five projects? Ten? Fifty? These assumptions can lead to creation of a unit cost, or hourly rate, for using the equipment that can be applied to a project estimate.

External labor costs and equipment costs are usually simpler to figure out. This is because contractors have already figured out what their costs for products or services are ahead of time and have provided a contract that's specific to the project. Sometimes, these rates can be negotiated. Under a cost-plus contract, the labor and equipment rates are written into the contract and the vendor bills the project for the amount of labor, equipment, and materials supplied to the project. Once this has been figured out, add it to the overall cost estimate for the budget.

The final piece to consider is the cost of materials. Material costs will vary widely depending on the nature of the project. The range can expand from materials needed to construct a building to the materials needed to develop software. The percentage of the total costs attributed to materials varies just as widely. The first place to look for the expected costs of materials is in the product specification or service plan.

Once the project's schedule and costs have been determined, it's possible to generate a cash-flow projection. Again, it is important to realize that estimating the costs that go into the budget is the responsibility of all of the project stakeholders. A cooperative approach yields more accurate results and helps to reduce the uncertainty of the project.

PROJECT RISK ASSESSMENT

Next, it is time to manage the project's risk. Not many project managers realize that managing risk is their primary responsibility, but they tend to do it without even thinking about it. Risk management is the total process to identify, control, and minimize the impact of uncertain events. The objective of the risk management program is to systematically reduce risk to increase the likelihood of having the project objectives met. In effect, as project managers know, all project management is risk management. As mentioned earlier, outside obstacles are assessed and accounted for when planning the project.

Project definition takes into account a lot of risk management activities. The project definition establishes the goals and constraints for the project. In this process, it is critical to identify the risks and the sources of such risk and then develop a response to that risk by examining the potential damage and the degree of likelihood of that risk occurring.

PROJECT PLAN AND STAGE GATES

The end of this whole process is a solid project plan, and it's also the transition into implementation of the project plan and movement of the project through its first "stage gate," a series of milestones for the project.

Project managers are increasingly using a stage gate approach. A stage gate specifically refers to a series of decision points (gates) for evaluating whether the project should continue to the next stage. This method brings a lot of focus on the viability of the project's outcome and, by providing the opportunity to "fail fast," allows the organization to pivot, modify, or abandon the project if needed. This method is generally more cost effective, because viability is serially determined rather than having to wait until the entire project (and its budget) has run its course.

In the stage gate approach, reaching the first stage gate also means the beginning of the second stage. Once sign off and agreement about the success of the first stage is reached, the project will pass through that stage gate and move into the second stage. When the second stage is completed and is put through a "go or no go" evaluation, it moves through the second stage gate;

this cycle continues through the stages and each stage's gate until the project is either completed, changed, or abandoned.

Close-out reporting is possibly the most neglected activity in project management. When the project is complete, it is tempting to have the final product speak for itself. What has been found, however, is that closing-out activities can bring a high return to the project managers. The closing out of a project can bring closure to the project in the eyes of the stakeholders, and they can also provide an excellent learning opportunity. It provides an opportune time to take a poll of the project participants and find out how they perceived the process.

One way to keep all of these learning points from surfacing all at once at the end of the project is to measure the progress of the project. This is also referred to as project control. Part of successfully controlling a project is to have project performance measures. These measures indicate when tasks have been accomplished and help you to measure whether you've completed what you thought you would by the dates previously established.

SUMMARY

Project management in its simplest form of understanding is all about planning and that it's somewhat complicated, and to do it well takes really delving into what needs to be done from the very beginning.

Although the practice of project management has been around for centuries, scholars and project management professionals are still studying how to make project management better. The value of face-to-face interaction does not deteriorate, even with the deployment of virtual project management teams. Projects require leaders that are trained in both business and technology and a team that has qualified project management professionals when possible. There are a variety of preferences and cultural values that weigh different communication techniques and interpersonal skills differently. Perceptions of communication techniques will have an impact on the end user and the end result of the project, so it is important to clarify preferences at the beginning. Perceptions of interpersonal skills can impact the success of the project managers as well as each of the team members on their performance evaluations.

Chapter 12

MANAGEMENT INFORMATION SYSTEMS

H ow have management information systems and information technology had such a profound impact on business? Maybe the better question to ask is has information technology changed business or has business actually created information technology? Surprisingly, if we take a historic look at business, it's actually less about technology and more about competition: a continued focus on increased productivity and efficiency has intensified competition and driven business toward technology.

Today's executives see how technology plays a key role in day-to-day operations. In fact, some businesses no longer even have a tangible presence but rather only exist virtually. The transformation from brick and mortar businesses into e-business has leveled off, but the role of technology and management information systems in business is undeniable. In this chapter, we will focus on the essentials needed to grow and compete in today's cyber environment and technology-driven organizations through the deployment of management information systems ("MIS").

Management Information Systems can be described as tools that help managers organize and make decisions from their data. More simply, effective MIS aids communication. Unsurprisingly, it's still true that people generally accomplish more together than they do apart, and the old concept of collaboration and communication is still at the core of business. Management information systems strive to efficiently collect, format, and communicate information to a wide variety of people using increasingly sophisticated software packages and applications using increasingly sophisticated and powerful hardware and networked systems.

THE HARDWARE

Computer hardware is a term used to identify the tools that we typically see when looking at someone's desk or see an executive in action: computer, monitor, keyboard, mouse, smartphone, scanner, or printer. There are also the components inside hardware that store and process the data that is entered into the systems.

Computers range from "mainframe" computers to smartphones. Mainframe computers are large installations mainly used to manage bulk data processing—they are very powerful and very expensive. Today, smartphones are bringing incredible levels of computing power into our pockets.

THE SOFTWARE

The real power and utility of the hardware is largely a function of the software. The most fundamental software is the operating system. The operating system (OS) executes commands, coordinates and provides instructions so the computer will deploy other "applications software" programs with specific functions and purpose, such as creating a financial spreadsheet/statement/model, preparing a slide presentation, or writing a document on a word-processing program. Specific "applications software" includes programs such as Microsoft's Word (word processing), PowerPoint (presentations), and Excel (spreadsheets).

Managing the hardware and software that are used in any business is a difficult task that requires highly specialized training about both hardware and software that's constantly and dramatically changing.

THE ROLE OF THE CHIEF INFORMATION OFFICER (CIO)

Small-business owners and most professionals are not large enough to justify having a CIO on board, but for larger organizations, the Chief Information Officer, or CIO, is the person in the company responsible for managing all the information collected from the various hardware and software applications and making sure that the information and communication flow is sufficient to meet the needs of the company objectives. CIOs are on board in an organization to determine the answers to the following questions:

- Is the organization leveraging IT in its most important business initiatives?
- Is management and shareholder information of the highest accuracy and integrity?
- Is the organization leveraging technology to ensure business continuity?
- Is the organization getting the best return on technology expenditures?
- Is the workforce using and managing information and technology effectively?
- Is the organization leveraging IT for business innovation and learning?
- Is the organization maximizing the potential of the Internet?
- Does the organization have the right IT partners?

MANAGEMENT INFORMATION SYSTEMS FOR DECISION-MAKING

While MIS is used most commonly for communications, the ultimate goal is to use these tools to help make better decisions. DSS, or decision support systems for example, are management information systems that quickly provide relevant data to help people choose a particular course of action. For example, a DSS tool may be able to simulate a situation and predict various outcomes based on known variables. What will the revenue of an airline be given the possible number of flights completed, taking into consideration weather delays and other unforeseen obstacles? How many passengers will be on each flight? How many seats at what prices? A DSS can take into account all of these variables and come up with various revenue projections based on the possible outcomes. These tools might be complicated to figure out at first, but they may prove to be invaluable in the long run for the amount of time and monetary resources saved.

CYBER SECURITY AS A KEY CHALLENGE FOR MIS SYSTEMS

As noted, e-mail is an extremely valuable tool that has found a secure place in today's business environment, but it has significant limitations with regards to privacy, piracy, and filtering. Not only is there a privacy/security risk via e-mail but computer crime, cyber terrorism, and viruses all pose a threat to operating systems.

Intellectual property can be the most valuable part of any business, and as an intangible asset it is also extremely difficult to protect. Just as computers and software programs offer efficient ways of communicating, they also provide gateways to unintended/illegal information sharing that is difficult to monitor.

An FBI survey presented disturbing results that showed 15 percent of businesses didn't know whether their systems had been attacked the previous year. And of those who reported that they had had attacks on their system, more than half of them never reported it to anyone.

Just as crime on the street has law enforcement officers monitoring and trying to control it, so does computer crime. Employees or outsiders can change or invent data in computing programs to produce inaccurate or misleading information or illegal transactions, or they can insert and spread viruses.

There are also malicious hackers who access computer systems for their own illicit benefit or knowledge…or just to see if they can get in. Hackers deploy a Trojan horse, which allows them to take over a computer without detection, leading to identity theft, international money laundering, theft of business trade secrets, auction fraud, website spoofing, and cyber extortion.

Because viruses are frequently spread through e-mail, it is important to know who the sender is before opening the message or an attachment and to use antivirus software to see if the document has a virus.

Other computer crimes consist of actual theft of computing equipment (laptops and smartphones are particularly vulnerable due to their small size), using computer technology to counterfeit currency or other official documents (passports, visas, ID cards, etc.), and using computer technology to illegally download or "pirate" music and movies that are copyrighted. With so much potential for computer crime, what can be done? If a security breach is suspected, the US Department of Homeland Security suggests taking the following steps:

- Respond quickly.
- Don't stop system processes or tamper with files if unsure of what actions to take.
- Use the telephone to communicate.
- Contact the incident response team at the bank or other financial institution.
- Establish contact points with general counsel, emergency response staff, and law enforcement.
- Identify a primary point of contact to handle potential evidence.
- Don't contact the suspected perpetrator.

In addition, it is important to prevent access to your system and viewing of data by unauthorized users by adopting practices of utilizing complex and often-changing passwords, firewalls, and encryption software.

Finally, it is critical to back up data and computing systems in case your system is attacked. There are many systems and ways for backing up data that provide safety, but the most important thing is that they be used consistently.

INTERNET, INTRANET, AND EXTRANET

As businesses and professional practices implement the use of technology and management information systems, it becomes important to link these tools together and provide a means for the machines, the information they produce, and those who use and benefit from the system to communicate with each other. Thus, computers in an organization and computers in different organizations form "networks" to facilitate the exchange.

COMPUTER NETWORKS AND THEIR IMPORTANCE

Computing systems consist of hardware and software and also networks. Local area networks (LAN) have the capacity to connect computers to the network from one physical site in the company's offices and within different buildings. At the designated site, people can share both the hardware and software of the system set up in that location.

LANs are changing, and today, wireless application (WLAN) provides the benefits of networking equipment without the use of cables and hardwiring. Before deciding which is best, consider the number of wireless access points, the type of information/data that will be transmitted, the speed needed for data transmission, the bandwidth that applications require, mobility coverage for roaming, and whether the system will be easily upgradeable as the technology advances.

A WLAN's speed as it appears upon purchase might not necessarily be the product's real-world speed, because the WLAN is a shared medium and divides available throughput rather than providing dedicated speeds to the connected devices as a dial-up connection would. This limitation makes it a little more challenging to figure out how much speed is needed; therefore, it is critical to purchase a model that is upgradeable.

Because wireless networks utilize technology that is a form of "broadcasting" data through the air, they present a security concern, so any system must include internal security measures in order to make sure the wireless data cannot be "hijacked" or hacked into by a cyber thief or pirate.

Throughput is a major consideration for wireless deployment. Consider what types of traffic—e-mail, web traffic, video, animation, graphics, speed-hungry ERP (enterprise resource planning) or CAD (computer-aided design) applications—will ride across the WLAN most often. Network speeds diminish significantly as users wander farther from their access points; thus, enough access points to support not only the number of users but the speeds at which they need to connect are required.

One certainty, however, is that with the advent of wireless, the requirement of sitting in one place connected to a wall to access the Internet is becoming obsolete. A virtual office is fast-becoming the organizational model for far-flung global enterprises.

CATEGORIES OF MANAGEMENT INFORMATION SYSTEMS

There are three primary MIS categories: transaction processing systems, management support systems, and office automation systems. Transaction processing systems handle daily business operations where they collect and organize operational data from the activities of the company. Management support systems are used to help analyze the data that is collected and organized and help make decisions by forecasting, generating reports, and performing other types of analysis. Office automation systems facilitate communication between people who use the same operating systems through word processing, e-mail, fax machines, and other types of technologies.

HOW COMPANIES MANAGE INFORMATION TECHNOLOGY TO THEIR ADVANTAGE

The first step in managing technology is to evaluate goals and objectives for the use of technology. It's critical to engage in a collaborative exploration among executives, IT managers, and stakeholders/users about specific needs and uses for proposed technology solutions. It is then useful to map the information flow to analyze how information is transferred from one point to another within an organization. While this concept itself is simple, it is important to understand that mapping the information flow will clarify the utility of a technology and align interests of internal users of a proposed technology solution.

Sometimes it's helpful to bring in outside expertise and perspectives about the deployment of technology. IT consultants specialize in helping organizations map their information flows and will likely propose an engagement with the following approach:

1. Describe the current situation. What does the company organization chart look like? Who are the "clients," or users of the system? Who *aren't* the clients but still use the system? Drill down even deeper to learn about such needs. Describe the potential clients in other business units within the company and discuss their specific information needs. This helps to give a better understanding of what information needs are, and are not, being met currently.
2. Mapping. This allows a visualization of the potential areas for overlap, potential for consolidation of resources, and new solutions for optimal information flow.
3. Rank the solutions for prioritization. This process helps decide which solution will meet the majority of needs while using the budgeted resources. The ranking process can be conducted by assessing the risk activity within the organization.
4. The final step in the process is then creating the information map. Mapping the final solutions to show each department and the suggestions for their information needs creates an understanding of each subset of the organization, highlights the ultimate client, and results in information solution recommendations for each.

TRENDS IN MANAGEMENT INFORMATION TECHNOLOGY

With antiquated "legacy" systems getting more and more expensive to fix, old computers breaking down, and the benefits of mobile computing continually being realized, new technology is entering the business world with increasing speed. As is often the case with the gradual diffusion of technological innovation into the marketplace, telecom and storage services are simultaneously decreasing in cost.

According to Michael J. Miller, the biggest growth opportunity for management information systems technology is in web services and software as a service (SaaS). He predicts that emerging web service standards will promote integration and let companies tie together existing applications within an organization, connect to outside applications, and create applications that are entirely new. Due to the increasing number of applications in the corporate world, Miller also does not see that just one player (such as Microsoft or Sun Microsystems) will dominate the market.

Noting the security issues discussed earlier, Miller sees that security is the biggest obstacle for continued growth in the sector and that both consumers and businesses will need to address issues of security better.

Another trend in MIS is business process management, which has spawned myriad applications and packages. BPM (business process management) is a fast-growing application of technology that finds its roots in automating the processes that involve people to produce high gains in productivity.

THE TALENT GAP IN MANAGEMENT INFORMATION SYSTEMS

While there's been a rush for adoption of technology, one of the associated needs has been to fill the shortage of people who can help integrate, install, and run these information systems. Companies are finding it increasingly difficult to stay current with the latest technologies. Seen as an excellent opportunity for the technology workforce, it can also be a competitive vulnerability for an organization that's missing the technology talent to leverage the value of management information systems.

Chapter 13

THE WEB AND THE "INTERNET OF THINGS"

Though it may be logical to include it in a discussion of management information systems, the importance of the Internet requires a chapter of its own, as it is the platform for e-commerce and the means by which a worldwide collection of computer networks cooperates with each other to exchange data and foster global commerce, knowledge, and communication.

Though considered by many as a "new" technology, the Internet has been around for several decades. Originally known as ARPAnet, the Internet was created in 1969 by the US Department of Defense as a nationwide computer network that would continue to operate even if the majority of it were destroyed in a nuclear war or natural disaster. It was not until 1992 that commercial entities started offering Internet access to the general public, and the world has not been the same since. Today, the pervasive use of the web has been termed "the Internet of things" that suggests that almost every point of contact between businesses, organizations, and their customers, clients, and stakeholders can benefit from some application of web-based technology and connectivity, and further, this collection of devices can be networked to exchange data, coordinate activities across devices, geographic boundaries in a coordinated, systematic manner. Think about how the automobile has become a "computer with wheels" capable of providing on-board data to a mechanic servicing the car who then, via the internet, uploads the data to a central knowledge base that results in actionable, efficient repair and service instructions. As the customer drops off the car at the repair shop, a map location pin is dropped that is emailed to a friend of the customer who uses a navigation system to find their way to the repair shop to pick up the customer and then the customer can track the friend's progress in driving to the repair shop.

THE EFFECT OF THE INTERNET ON BUSINESS

Widespread Internet and e-mail access has radically changed the way companies do business and communicate with their employees, vendors, and customers. Consumers and businesses purchase products and services such as laptops and airline tickets by paying with credit cards via the Internet without ever speaking to a customer representative or salesperson. Many companies allow customers to track the status of their orders online to see when their products shipped and when they are scheduled to arrive, again without ever speaking to a customer representative. When companies such as Amazon and Priceline emerged, their business models revolved around conducting 100 percent of their business online, eliminating the need for costly brick and mortar outlets. More and more consumers are paying their bills online as they become comfortable with online security, thus eliminating the need to pay postage and write checks for each bill using the traditional snail-mail method. Today, thousands of adults are getting their undergraduate and master's degrees online without ever attending an actual class or meeting their peers or professors, who teach the classes online. There are few businesses or organizations isolated from this transformational wave of technology and innovation.

THE CLOUD AND SOFTWARE AS A SERVICE (SAAS)

As the world becomes more interconnected, we live in an environment where the Internet and communication services are immediate and accessible. Organizations can communicate with their customers, stakeholders, employees, and the world almost instantly, and importantly, these all are accessible via a number of devices.

With current smartphone technology and broadband networks, incredible computing power is almost always with us in our office, in our car, in our pocket. This hyper-connectivity is acutely redefining relationships between consumers, individuals, enterprises, and governments while introducing new opportunities, challenges, and risks in terms in terms of access to information and flow of confidential data.

The term *cloud* refers to using the Internet for sharing and storing content and data. Instead of buying a software product on a disk or downloading a static copy of the program, Software as a Service (SAAS) is cloud-based, with the vendor providing continuous updates, maintenance, and access on a 24/7 subscription, rather than one-time purchase, basis.

Presented and utilized as an alternative to physical storage devices and expensive internal servers, cloud computing has emerged as a convenient method of accessing and sharing data. Whether on a large economic scale or something as compact as a smartphone, cloud computing is the answer to data collection and efficient modification of technology to suit the modern needs of a corporate world constantly looking for ease of access to information. The ability to scale according to use and demand presents a compelling reason for organizations to move their data from site specific hardware servers with a fixed amount of capacity to cloud-based data storage that can, as needed, expand or contract seamlessly.

In recent times, cloud computing has become extremely common and is the most preferred method of data storage and distribution, as it provides an ease of access reminiscent of science fiction stories. Cheap yet fast and very easily accessible through any portal that connects to the Internet, it is the method of choice for the current technologically advancing world. Large-scale and high-speed data collaboration becomes the norm on a global level, with cloud-based systems providing these benefits:

- Can scale to handle peaks and flows of workload
- No need to install hardware or software
- Lowers the cost of capital as servers and IT maintenance are not as needed or heavy-handed as before the application of cloud computing
- Provides economies of scale for organizations that may not otherwise afford a large internal database without significant expenditure
- Savings of costs for maintenance
- Less or even no time required for updating large-scale data
- Speedy access to information

THE EMERGENCE OF E-COMMERCE

While e-commerce is pervasive and well-accepted, adopters of online buying and selling are wary of its challenges.

One major concern is that consumers are fearful about security and privacy of personal information. Consumers want to be assured that personal information will not be sold to other companies for marketing purposes. Consumers are also wary about technology that tracks personal information such as websites visited and items purchased by customers. A major barrier for consumers who still do not purchase products online is the fear that a website is not secure and that their credit card number or other personal information will be accessed by hackers.

Another reason to avoid e-commerce is the frequency of viruses. While in the past viruses were often spread by opening infected e-mails, these days, simply surfing the Internet can make one vulnerable to getting a virus.

Although there are challenges associated with e-commerce, there are also many advantages to selling products online. One advantage for companies is cost savings through lower inventory management, customer service, administration, communication costs, order tracking, and integration with the company's accounting system.

Manufacturers of products have the advantage of being able to sell directly to customers, with larger margins than having intermediaries, middlemen, or wholesale distributors. Communicating with customers is as easy a click of the mouse, where spot promotions, limited time offers and other means of promotion can be launched and can reach the customer within minutes or seconds. Through management information systems with customer data, an organization has the opportunity to generate a low-cost, highly customized promotion to a well-defined customer segment. For the consumer, convenience, comparative shopping, and access to information represent major benefits, resulting in an ever-widening audience of online customers.

HARNESSING THE POWER OF A WEB "INSIDE"—CREATING A SUCCESSFUL INTRANET

The Internet is a global network of computers linked together, while an intranet is an internal, secured network within an organization that can only be accessed through a password by authorized users such as employees, existing clients, or customers.

The key advantage to implementing an intranet is improved communications; an intranet facilitates the sharing of knowledge between employees, collaboration on work-related documents, learning the latest company news, and socializing outside of work to form stronger bonds. Additionally, intranets can save companies money on printing, paper, and distribution costs. They can also increase productivity and efficiency. Allowing clients to access project and budget data, invoices, and old reports through a password is an example of an Intranet.

For example, if employee directories, benefits information (401(k), health insurance, etc.), holidays, upcoming events, company organizational charts, and policies are posted on the intranet, employees spend less time searching for paperwork or calling employees in other departments for answers to their questions.

Employees can also receive information regarding news and announcements simultaneously and in a timely manner rather than have to wait for the information to be announced in the next staff/team meeting or distributed in their internal mailboxes. This sharing of information makes employees feel like they are an important part of the organization. As a result of improved communications and efficiency, employees are more likely to be satisfied with their jobs and become more loyal to the company, thereby increasing employee retention and improving customer service. Especially in large, complex, global-reaching organizations, an intranet is a critical tool for sharing knowledge across the entire organization. An experience, a solution, a client that is beneficial to one unit in the organization may also have great value if shared with other units. Many issues and challenges in one area of an organization may have been met and resolved in another area, so knowledge-sharing via intranet can be a highly productive deployment of technology as simple as an electronic bulletin board or an organization's own "wiki" that provides any authorized visitor to update or view critical information in a database that is found on an organization's intranet

IMPLEMENTATION OF AN INTRANET

To ensure that an intranet is successful, the information on it must be consistent with the company's brand, business objectives, and mission. Additionally, enough staff and resources should be allocated to promote and implement the intranet as well as adequate staff to maintain and refresh it.

Incorporating intranet objectives in regular strategic planning helps to ensure that the intranet is aligned with the organization's goals and objectives each year. Ideally, a team approach that incorporates input from a diverse set of users' needs and perspectives will be gathered to review and refresh the intranet. The intranet strategist would monitor performance against objectives, track the budget and resources allocated to the project, and ensure that standard procedures are implemented in the layout of pages.

The success of an intranet not only depends on adequate staff, funding, and site content, but also on senior management buy-in. If senior management fails to actively support the intranet, it will be a challenge to convince others to use the system. If managers expect their employees to use the intranet, they must lead by example and use it themselves.

SUMMARY

Harnessing the power of the web and technology is a vital part of an organization's success and future. To remain competitive in today's business environment, companies must retain their employees, improve communications with clients and employees, improve productivity, increase efficiency, and reduce costs. Implementing an intranet and integrating the web into a strategic plan can help achieve these goals. While websites can be used as marketing and sales tools, they can also be used to improve internal organizational efficiency by streamlining the ordering, tracking, and vendor bidding processes. In today's complex, competitive world, technology can be a powerful element in attaining competitive advantage, lowering costs, increasing customer satisfaction, and achieving long-term success.

Chapter 14

QUALITY MANAGEMENT SYSTEMS

F or several decades, *quality* and *quality management systems* have been leading buzzwords in the business world. Numerous consultants have built their careers around these topics, and quality issues in business have been responsible for the development of new organizations and even industries—for instance, the American Society for Quality and Six Sigma Consulting.

The notion of quality in business focuses on the savings and additional revenue that organizations can realize if they eliminate errors throughout their operations and produce products and services at the optimal level of quality desired by their customers. Errors can take almost any form—producing the wrong number of parts, sending a bank statement to a customer who has already closed his or her account, or sending an incorrect bill to a client. All of these errors are very common, and the costs incurred seem minimal. Over time, however, when mistakes are repeated, the costs add up to a significant amount, which if corrected can result in significant increases to the bottom line.

WHAT IS QUALITY?

According to the American Society for Quality, the word *quality* can be defined in the following ways:

- Based on customers' perceptions of a product/service's design and how well the design matched the original specifications
- The ability of a product/service to satisfy stated or implied needs
- Achieved by conforming to established requirements within an organization

WHAT IS A QUALITY MANAGEMENT SYSTEM?

A quality management system is a management technique used to communicate to employees what is required to produce the desired quality of products and services and to influence employee actions to complete tasks and services. It should

- establish a vision for the employees;
- set standards for employees;
- build motivation within the company;
- set goals for employees;
- help fight the resistance to change within organizations; and
- help direct the corporate culture.

WHY IS QUALITY IMPORTANT?

Success may simply be the extent to which an organization can produce a higher quality product or service than its competitors are able to do at a competitive price. When quality is the key to a company's success, quality management systems allow organizations to keep up with and meet current quality levels, meet the consumer's requirement for quality, retain employees through competitive compensation programs, and keep up with the latest technology.

A HISTORY OF THE QUALITY MOVEMENT

As early as the 1950s, Japanese companies began to see the benefits of emphasizing quality throughout their organizations and enlisted the help of an

American, W. Edwards Deming, who is credited with giving Japanese companies a massive head start in the quality movement. His methods include statistical process control (SPC) and problem-solving techniques that were very effective in gaining the necessary momentum to change the mentality of organizations needing to produce high-quality products and services.

Deming believed that 85 percent of all quality problems were the fault of management. In order to improve, management had to take the lead and put in place the necessary resources and systems. For example, consistent quality in incoming materials could not be expected when buyers were not given the necessary tools to understand quality requirements of those products and services.

Buyers need to fully understand how to assess the quality of all incoming products and services, understand the quality requirements, and be able to communicate these requirements to vendors. In a well-managed quality system, buyers should also be allowed to work closely with vendors and help them meet or exceed the required quality requirements.

According to Deming, quality systems were needed to address two different concepts of process improvement: (1) common (systematic) causes of error, and (2) special causes of error. *Systematic causes* are errors shared by numerous personnel, machines, or products. *Special causes* are associated with individual employees or equipment. Systematic causes of errors include poor product/ service design, materials not suited for their use, improper bill of lading, and poor physical conditions. Special causes of errors include lack of training or skill, a poor lot of incoming materials, or equipment out of order.

Another influential individual in the development of quality control was Joseph M. Juran, who, like Deming, made a name for himself working in Japanese organizations that were focused on improving quality. Juran established the Juran Institute in 1979; its goals and objectives were centered on helping organizations improve the quality of their products and services.

Juran defined quality as "fitness for use," meaning that the users of products or services should be able to rely on that product or service 100 percent of the time without any worry of defects. If this was true, the product could be classified as fit for use.

Quality of design could be described as what distinguishes a Yugo from a Mercedes Benz and involves the design concept and specifications. The quality of a product or service is only as good as its design and intention. Thus, it is important to include quality issues in the design process, as well as keeping in mind during the design phase the difficulties one might have in replicating the product or service with the intended quality level.

Quality of conformance is reflected in the ability to replicate each aspect of a product or service with the same quality level as that intended in the design. This responsibility is held by individuals to develop the processes for replication then by the workforce, their training, supervision, and adherence to protocols that ensure consistency and conformity.

Availability refers to freedom from disruptive problems throughout the process and is measured by the frequency or probability of defects—for example, if a process does not have a steady flow of electricity, which causes defective parts, or when an employee must complete two jobs at once and is therefore forced to make concessions on the quality of both products or services.

Safety is described by Juran as calculating the risk of injury due to product hazards. For example, even if the product or service meets or exceeds all quality standards and expectations, if there is a possibility that it could injure someone if not used properly, the product will not be considered high quality.

Field use refers to the ability of the product to reach the end user with the desired level of quality. This involves packaging, transportation, storage and field service competence, and promptness.

Juran also developed a comprehensive approach to quality that spanned a product or service's entire life cycle, from design to customer relations and all the steps in between. Juran preached that an organization should dissect all processes and procedures from a quality perspective and analyze for a "fitness for use." Once this is completed, the organization can begin to make changes based on the "fitness for use" model.

THE QUALITY REVOLUTION COMES TO THE UNITED STATES

The push for increased quality began in American manufacturing companies in the 1980s, following in the footsteps of Japanese manufacturers. Japanese companies found themselves with a distinct competitive advantage over American companies with their ability to produce much higher-quality products with fewer defects.

The Ford Motor Company was the first to invite Deming to help the company transform itself into a quality-oriented organization. As a result, the company was able to achieve higher quality standards than any other American automotive manufacturer and substantial sales growth in the late 1980s, even when the rest of the US automotive market was declining. Ford attributes the ability of its Taurus to overtake the Honda Accord in annual sales to high quality standards set by the company.

Congress, seeing the need for American companies to strive for increased quality, established the Malcolm Baldrige National Quality Award, modeled after Japan's Deming Prize. This spawned a substantial increase in the resources American businesses allocated for quality improvement, and within ten years, an American organization was able to capture Japan's Deming Prize for quality.

Since the early 1980s and on into the twenty-first century, quality issues have surfaced in every industry and almost every organization in the United States. The quality movement started in manufacturing and then moved to service industries. Initially, service organizations did not feel quality systems would transfer very easily from manufacturing, but service companies today are reaping substantial rewards from implementing quality programs.

Throughout the history of the quality movement, there have been several approaches to quality and even the development of several organizations dedicated solely to setting standards for quality.

STANDARDIZED SYSTEMS

ISO 9000 is a series of quality management systems (QMS) standards created by the International Organization for Standardization (ISO), a federation of 132 national standards bodies. The ISO 9000 QMS standards are not specific to products or services but apply to the processes that create them. The standards are generic in nature so that they can be used by manufacturing and service industries anywhere in the world.

An organization that would like to be certified by the ISO needs to meet all the criteria stated in the ISO standards and pass a detailed audit performed by an ISO auditor. In some industries, ISO certification has become necessary; for example, some large manufacturers require all suppliers to be ISO certified. Although ISO certification is very respected, if it is not a trend in your specific industry, the additional cost of certification is a deterrent to most managers. It is very possible to reach the desired quality level within an organization with a well-planned quality system and without going through all the additional steps for ISO certification.

TOTAL QUALITY MANAGEMENT (TQM)

TQM is a management approach in which quality is emphasized in every aspect of the business and organization. Its goals are aimed at long-term development of quality products and services. TQM breaks down every process or activity and emphasizes that each contributes or detracts from the quality and productivity of the organization as a whole.

Management's role in TQM is to develop a quality strategy that is flexible enough to be adapted to every department, aligned with the organizational business objectives, and based on customer and stakeholder needs. Once the strategy is defined, it must be the motivating force to be deployed and communicated for it to be effective at all levels of the organization.

Some degree of employee empowerment is also encompassed in the TQM strategy and usually involves both departmental and cross-functional teams developing strategies to solve quality problems and make suggestions for improvement.

CONTINUOUS QUALITY IMPROVEMENT (CQI)

Continuous Quality Improvement came into existence in manufacturing as a different approach to quality and quality systems. It does not focus as much on creating a corporate quality culture, but more on the process of quality improvement by the deployment of teams or groups that are rewarded when goals and quality levels are reached. CQI allows individuals involved in the day-to-day operations to change and improve processes and work flows as they see fit.

CQI implementation attempts to develop a quality system that is never satisfied; it strives for constant innovation to improve work processes and systems by reducing time-consuming, low-value-added activities. The time and resource savings can now be devoted to planning and coordination.

CQI has been adapted in several different industries. For example, in health care and other service sectors, it has taken on the acronym FOCUS-PDCA work, which stands for the following steps:

- Find a process to improve
- Organize to improve a process
- Clarify what is known

- Understand variation
- Select a process improvement

Then move through the process improvement plan:

- Plan—create a timeline, including all resources, activities, dates, and personnel training
- Do—implement the plan and collect data
- Check—analyze the results of the plan
- Act—act on what was learned and determine the next steps

The FOCUS-PDCA acronym is an easy system for management to communicate to teams, and it helps them stay organized and on track with the end result in mind. The system has proven to be very successful for the CQI team approach.

SIX SIGMA

Six Sigma was developed at Motorola in the 1980s as a method to measure and improve high-volume production processes. Its overall goal was to measure and eliminate waste by attempting to achieve near perfect results. The term *Six Sigma* refers to a statistical measure with no more than 3.4 defects per million. Numerous companies, including General Electric, Ford, and DaimlerChrysler, have credited Six Sigma with saving them billions of dollars.

Six Sigma is a statistically oriented approach to process improvement that uses a variety of tools, including Statistical Process Control (SPC), Total Quality Management (TQM), and Design of Experiments (DOE). It can be coordinated with other major initiatives and systems, such as new product development, Materials Requirement Planning (MRP), and Just-In-Time (JIT) Inventory Control.

Six Sigma was initially thought of as a system that could only be used in manufacturing operations, but more recently it has been proven to be successful in non-manufacturing processes as well, such as accounts payable, billing, marketing, and information systems.

At first glance, Six Sigma might seem too structured to be effective in analyzing processes that are not standard and repetitive as in manufacturing situations, but the theory of Six Sigma is flexible enough to suit any process. Nevertheless, many of the lessons learned on production lines are very relevant to other processes as well. The Six Sigma process consists of the following steps, which can be completed once the business breaks down the process flow into individual steps:

- Define what defects there are
- Measure the number of defects
- Probe for the root cause
- Implement changes to improve
- Remeasure
- Take a long-term view of goals

ELEMENTS OF A QUALITY SYSTEM

There are several elements to a quality system, and each organization's system will be unique. The most important elements of a quality system include participative management, quality system design, customers, purchasing, education and training, statistics, auditing, and technology.

PARTICIPATIVE MANAGEMENT

The entire quality process, once started, will be an ongoing dynamic part of the organization, just like any other department such as marketing or accounting. It will also need the continuous focus of management. The implementation and management of a successful quality system involves many different aspects that must be addressed on a continuous basis.

VISION AND VALUES

The starting point for the management and leadership process is the formation of a well-defined vision and value statement. This statement will be used to establish the importance of the quality system and build motivation for the changes that need to take place, whether the organization plans to exceed customer expectations, commit to a defined level of customer satisfaction, or commit to zero defects. The exact form of the vision and values statement is not as important as the fact that it is articulated and known by everyone involved. This statement is going to be a driving force to help mold the culture that is needed throughout the organization in the drive for quality. It is not the words of the vision and values statement that produce quality products and services; it is the people and processes that determine if there is going be a change in quality. The statement plays a large part in setting agendas for all other processes used to manage the quality system.

DEVELOPING THE PLAN

The plan for the quality system will be different for every organization, but there are similar characteristics:

- Clear and measurable goals
- Financial resources available for quality
- Consistent with the organization's vision and values

The plan for the quality system might also include pilot projects that would entail setting up small, quality projects within the organization. This will allow management to understand how well the quality system is accepted, learn from mistakes, and have greater confidence in launching an organization-wide quality system.

The plan should provide some flexibility for employee empowerment, because, as has been demonstrated, the most successful quality systems allow employees at all levels to provide input.

COMMUNICATION

Change, especially a movement toward higher quality, is challenging to communicate effectively, yet the communication process is essential for the company's leaders to move the organization forward. Communication is the vital link between management, employees, consumers, and stakeholders. These communication lines also bring about a sense of camaraderie between all individuals involved and help sustain the drive for the successful completion of long-term quality goals.

Communication systems also must allow for employees to give feedback and provide possible solutions to issues the company must face. Management needs to allow for this in both formal and informal ways, such as employee feedback slips and feedback roundtable meetings.

The responsibility for fostering a culture that values communication lies with senior management. They alone have to ensure that goals and objectives are communicated to all. They are also responsible for setting up the system for feedback from the employees.

REWARDS AND ACKNOWLEDGMENT

Rewards, compensation, and acknowledgment for achievements in quality are very effective ways to motivate employees. They tell employees exactly what management is trying to accomplish at the end of the day. Rewards, compensation, and acknowledgment may also be seen as a form of communication—they are tangible methods that senior management uses to let employees know that quality is important. This could come in the form of individual rewards or team rewards.

Rewards, compensation, and acknowledgement may take many forms, and it is up to management to ensure that this type of program is in line with the goals and objectives of the quality system and the goals and objectives of the organization. Organizations have found that the best and most cost-effective programs are geared to meeting specific criteria. These programs motivate managers who, in turn, motivate their employees to strive toward predefined goals.

QUALITY SYSTEM DESIGN

A quality system is composed of the standards and procedures that are developed to ensure that the level of quality desired is repeated in every unit of a product or service. This portion of the quality system is very concrete and can be measured and managed. Before it's started, the organization should establish a core team to carry the performance system design process forward. The design process consists of eight steps:

1. Understand and map all business structures and processes. This forces employees involved in designing a performance measurement system to think through and understand the entire organization, its competitive position, the environment in which it operates, and its business processes. This will also allow for complete understanding of customer touch points and how the different operations in the organization affect the customer's perception of quality.

2. Develop business performance priorities. The performance measurement system should support the stakeholders' requirements from the organization's strategy through to its business processes. This order of priorities must be in place well before the process enters the actual design phase.

3. Understand the current performance measurement system. Every organization has some kind of measurement system in place. For this reason, there are basically two ways to approach the design and implementation of a new performance measurement system. It can either

scrap the old system and introduce a new one as a replacement, or it can redevelop the existing system. Both approaches can work, but the former approach is more likely to lead to trouble. People will cling to the old measurement system and either use both systems simultaneously or use the old one and simply go through the motions of the new one. The organization can eliminate this outcome by taking the second approach.

4. Develop performance indicators. The most important element of a performance measurement system is the set of performance indicators used to measure the organization's performance and processes. This is the point in the design process where the top-down approach meets the bottom-up design approach and where the broad masses of the organization become involved. The purpose of this step is to develop the performance measurement system with an appropriate number of relevant and accurate performance indicators.

5. Decide how to collect the required data. Developing perfect performance indicators about what goes on in the organization is one thing, but being able to collect the data required to calculate these performance indicators is a completely different matter. This issue must initially be addressed during the development of the performance indicators to avoid selecting those that can never actually be measured. There will be trade-offs of cost and time versus the benefits of collecting data, but a likely middle ground between perfect data/high cost and no data/no cost will be found.

6. Design reporting and performance data representation formats. In this step, decide how the performance data will be presented to the users; how the users should apply the performance data for management, monitoring, and improvement; and who will have access to performance data. Upon completion, the organization should have a performance measurement system that has a solid place in its overall measurement-based management system.

7. Test and adjust the performance measurement system. The first attempt at the performance measurement system will probably not be

perfect—there are bound to be performance indicators that do not work as intended, conflicting indicators, undesirable behavior, and problems with data availability. This is to be expected. In this step, extensively test the system and adjust the elements that do not work as planned.

8. Implement the performance measurement system. Now it's time to put the system to use. This is when the system is officially in place and everyone can start using it. This step involves issues such as managing user access, training, and demonstrating the system.

This is not an absolute process that needs to be followed to the letter in order for it to work. In some cases, one or more steps may be unnecessary; in others, additional steps may be needed. It's up to the leadership of the organization to make the necessary adjustments to the process to maximize the probability of the system's success.

DESIGNING PART TWO OF THE QUALITY SYSTEM

This portion of the quality system is conceptual. It is more about management's role in increasing motivation and the determination to make the first part run smoothly. It is rooted in the communication between management and employees, which was discussed earlier. In most cases, the employees who are performing the activities and process know how to improve the quality. This part of the system should allow employees to make recommendations and motivate them to want to improve quality.

CUSTOMERS

The inclusion of customers in a quality program can take many different avenues, including the cost of losing a customer, the customer's perception of quality, and the satisfaction level of the customers. The customer portion of a quality program is going to be unique for every industry and organization, but it must capture how quality plays into the customer's value system and how quality drives the purchase decision.

In service industries in particular, quality is measured in customer retention rates and the cost of losing a customer. If typical accounting measures could capture the exact cost of losing a customer, it would be easy for managers to allocate the exact amount of resources needed to retain customers. According to the *Harvard Business Review,* organizations can increase profits by almost 100 percent by retaining 5 percent more of their customers. Customers over time will generate more profits the longer they stay with the same company.

Perceived quality by customers leads to referrals; in service industries, referrals can equate to more than 60 percent of new business. If a company can increase the number of referrals through increased quality, it is going to have a substantial effect on the bottom line of the business.

PURCHASING

Purchasing is an area in an organization where substantial gains in quality can be realized through the implementation of just a few policies and procedures designed around quality. Today's suppliers need to be partners in the quality effort. A company's products or services are only as good as the combination of all the inputs.

The first step in molding the purchasing system to collaborate with the entire quality system is to take all the standards developed for all incoming materials that can be qualified as an input to routine process or activity. If the quality system's performance standards and procedures are completed as described in the design phase, these standards should already be established.

The second step is educating the purchasing personnel on how the standards are important to the process flows of the organization. If standards are not upheld, the quality of the product or service will be jeopardized. The employees should also be educated on how to measure and communicate the required standards. This may involve materials or statistical process control education, and it could even be as simple as cross-training the purchasing personnel so that they know exactly how the inputs fit into the organization. Once the purchasing area knows how the products are used and what problems can arise, they will have a better chance of procuring inputs that meet all the specifications.

Once steps one and two are complete, it will be the purchasing department's responsibility to communicate the requirements to suppliers and hold them accountable for the quality. This may not always be a simple task and could involve finding new suppliers or working with current suppliers to develop higher quality standards.

EDUCATION AND TRAINING

The education of employees for the purpose of reaching higher quality standards has many different facets. For example, the quality education of management is going to be different than the quality education of the general workforce because they play different roles in the process.

Because most quality problems start at the top, so too should education. The education of management on quality issues should start with a general discussion of quality systems and the roles management plays in quality programs.

With respect to general knowledge, management must understand the history of the quality movement, who the major players were, and how quality programs have affected the business world. More specifically, managers must know how quality programs have affected their specific industry in the past, and they should have an idea of what role quality programs play in the future of their industry.

Management must also keep abreast of new developments in quality. The discussion of the roles that management must play in a quality system is the most important aspect of their education. Management must understand how employees view their actions or inactions, how individual actions and jobs impact quality, and the overall importance of dedication to quality by management. Managers must understand that without strong leadership and reinforcing dedication to quality, a quality program will not be meaningful.

The education of employees for a quality program will include a discussion of how these programs will affect their job on a daily basis. It should also include a brief overview of quality as well as the tools they will use in order to ensure outputs and how their roles add to the overall quality goals of the organization.

DATA DEVELOPMENT AND STATISTICS

Statistical analysis is a very important aspect of quality systems. It could be considered a cornerstone of the quality improvement process and is very closely tied to auditing a quality system, which is discussed later in the chapter. A very common phrase in management, which relates well to quality, is "you cannot manage what you cannot measure," and statistical analysis will provide the measurements necessary to make management decisions. Statistics was a key tool that Deming used to distinguish between systemic and special causes, and the key to quality management in general was statistical process control.

AUDITING

Auditing a quality management system is just as important as any other aspect of the system. The audit process allows everyone involved to see if the quality management system is working correctly and if the goals and objectives are being reached. Auditing also plays major roles in motivating employees and allows for rewards and acknowledgment measures to be assessed as well as possible compensation.

Auditing of quality management systems can take many forms, and each organization will have a unique auditing process that fits its system. Service industries will have a very different auditing system from that of manufacturing organizations, but the end result of the systems will be the same. Some examples of auditing systems used in service organizations include mystery shoppers, customer surveys, and quality in service.

Mystery shoppers

Mostly used in quality assessment for retail stores and personal services, anonymous shoppers or clients are sent to retail stores, restaurants, medical practices, hair salons, and so on to interact with employees, assess the overall service quality, and report back to management. This is usually done on a regular basis, and reports are produced for the employees.

Customer surveys

Customer surveys are now used fairly often as a means to find out how an organization is viewed by customers. These surveys may take the form of mail-in forms or short forms consumers complete at the time of purchase or online, or a store may even have a salesperson or clerk ask the customer to rate the product or service at the close of the purchase. Getting direct input from customers is invaluable and should be done in some form in every organization.

Quality in services

Quality in service industries has more recently come into the mainstream, and the benefits reaped by service organizations initiating solid quality management programs have been substantial. The basis for quality management systems in service organizations is to proactively measure and manage the quality level of the services.

Many service organizations are aware of the iceberg principle. Like an iceberg, where only a small portion of the danger is visible, the average service company never hears from more than 90 percent of its customers who are not happy with the level of service they received, and the damage gets more worrisome:

- For every legitimate complaint received, there will be more than twenty customers who feel they have had problems, and at least 25 percent of those problems could be considered serious enough to warrant investigation.
- Of the customers who make a complaint, more than half will do business again if the complaint is addressed and resolved. If the complaint is resolved quickly and the customer feels the organization cares about its customers, the number will jump up to almost 100 percent.
- If a complaint is not resolved, the average customer will tell more than eight other individuals about his or her negative experience. If the complaint is resolved, however, and the experience is a positive one, that number decreases to five.
- On average, it costs six times more to gain a new customer than to keep an existing one.

It's easy to understand why quality in service industries can have substantial influence on the bottom line. A well-designed and managed quality system can be the key to providing the quality of service desired.

SUMMARY

The quality movement and quality systems have had many different names in the past few decades. It might look like a short-lived business-management trend at first glance. With ever-increasing competition and consumer expectations, professionals and business managers cannot ignore quality issues and expect to maintain or improve their competitive position. Quality systems have been responsible for substantial increases in the bottom line of businesses in every industry and have given organizations the boost they need to meet overall goals and objectives. Organizations that do not accept that quality improvement is going to be ingrained into every part of their business are not going to be around to see what the future brings.

Made in the USA
Monee, IL
18 June 2023